A Journey to Faith

George Austin has been Archdeacon of York since 1988 and is a frequent broadcaster, regularly appearing on Radio 4's 'Thought for the Day'. He was born in Bury, Lancashire, and ordained in 1956, after university at St David's College, Lampeter and training at Chichester Theological College. Over the years he has ministered in a variety of places, including Notting Hill, London University, Dunstable and Eaton Bray, Bedfordshire. Before being made Archdeacon he was the Vicar of Bushey Heath, near Watford, for eighteen years. He has been married to Bobbie for thirty years and they have a grown-up son, Jeremy, who is a journalist.

George Austin

A Journey to Faith

TRi△NGlE

First published 1992

Triangle
SPCK
Holy Trinity Church
Marylebone Road
London NW1 4DU

British Library Cataloguing in Publication Data

A catalogue record for this book is available
from the British Library.

ISBN 0-281-04600-X

Typeset by Inforum Typesetting, Portsmouth
Printed and bound in Great Britain by
BPCC Hazells Ltd
Member of BPCC Ltd

To Bobbie and Jeremy

A Meditation

God has created me to do Him some definite service,
    He has not committed to another.
I have a mission – I may never know it in this life,
    but I shall be told it in the next.
I am a link in a chain,
    a bond of connection between persons.
He has not created me for naught.
I shall do good, I shall be an angel of peace,
    a preacher of truth in my own place
    while not intending it
– if I do but keep His commandments.

Therefore I will trust Him.
Whatever, wherever I am.
If I am in sickness,
    my sickness may serve Him;
If I am in perplexity,
    my perplexity may serve Him;
If I am in sorrow;
    my sorrow may serve Him.
He does nothing in vain.
He knows what He is about.
He may take away my friends,
He may throw me among strangers,
He may make me desolate, make my spirits sink,
    hide my future from me,
– still, He knows what He is about.

John Henry Newman

Contents

Chapter one

The Family

I was born on Thursday, 16th July 1931, in the workhouse at Jericho. Lest that should qualify me for automatic membership of Board for Social Responsibility working parties as the token pauper/token Palestinian, perhaps I ought to explain.

Jericho is a suburb of Bury in Lancashire, and by 1931 the old workhouse had been reborn as the new maternity hospital. But it remained a place of dark malignancy for the older inhabitants of the town, and to her dying day my grandmother, on those rarest of occasions when she lost an argument, would burst into tears and cry out, in a bitter accusation uttered loudly enough (so she hoped) for the neighbours to hear: 'You're going to send a poor old woman to end her days in Jericho!'

Poor she was not, by the standards of those poor days. Her husband, Jack Austin, had drunk himself to a merciful death in 1918 and my father, then only eighteen years of age and about to be conscripted into the Royal Navy, found himself the inheritor of the princely sum of £2,000. Grandfather Jack had died intestate and so, under the law of that day, the estate went to the eldest (in this case, the only) son. My father, in the idealism of youth, thought this to be wrong and at once passed on the whole amount to his mother, who rewarded him in later life with frequent charges that he was trying 'to do her out what was hers.'

Grandma bought six terraced houses in Alfred Street, another four in Laurel Street, and a more modern corner terrace across the road from 10 Heywood Street South, where we lived with her and under her thumb until 1949. Some time during or after the war, Heywood Street South was renamed as the more genteel Parkhills Road, and overnight we joined the middle classes. But that is to anticipate: what about the Family?

On 10th September 1929, Oswald Hulton Austin married Evelyn (Ev-lynn, never *Ee*ve-lyn) Twigg in Rochdale Road Baptist Church, also known – rather irritatingly to other clergy of the town – as 'Christian Church', where the Twiggs worshipped. Both had been born in 1900, Evelyn being some three months his junior. At that time her father, George Twigg, was honorary organist at Christian Church and was known locally as a composer of many 'heart-stirring hymn tunes'.

But in 1903, George and Caroline Twigg, with their tiny daughter Evelyn, took on a great adventure and sailed from Liverpool to the United States, intending to settle in New England. Two years later they were back in Bury, where George was to die suddenly and painfully of a twisted bowel. He is mentioned alongside another young colleague in a contemporary account of the activities of Christian Church by its pastor as 'two of the finest characters I have ever met with. Earnest, sincere, humble, devout and Christ-like. We expected much from their continuance in our midst, but God wanted them for higher service. Of the many noble young men raised in Christian Church never have there been better than these worthy sons of worthy sires.' There have been moments in my life when I have felt that Grandfather George Twigg has not been far away, encouraging, strengthening and supporting.

A year or so after his death, mother and daughter were back again in New England, in Providence, Rhode Island and Orange, Massachusetts, where Caroline is said to have become engaged. Maybe there is a sad story there, for she returned – unwed – to England and Bury with Evelyn, now twelve years of age. So before she was thirteen, my mother had crossed the Atlantic four times in conditions hard to imagine in these days of easy transatlantic flight.

Evelyn proved to be intelligent and quick with her fingers,

2

never losing her skills as a needlewoman, or in knitting and crochet, and when she left school at fourteen she became a milliner. A year later, she came home from work one day and told her mother she had met such a nice boy – and promptly burst into tears. It was my father. Not surprisingly, widow Twigg was more than a little anxious. Evelyn was a devout Baptist, soon to become a full member, and as nonconformists they were of course teetotal by total conviction. And Ossie Austin was the son of the landlord of first the Clay Bank public house in Rochdale Road and later the more prestigious Hare and Hounds hotel in the centre of the town. Jack Austin had played football for Newton Heath (later to become Manchester United) and was known to have broken a man's leg in a fierce tackle. And he more than liked his booze. Even the fact that Ossie had once won a Temperance Society certificate for writing an essay on the evils of drink (about which, as he was to say afterwards, he knew more than any of the other lads at school) did not lessen Caroline Twigg's concern, any more than did Jack's framing of the certificate and placing it over the public bar.

Even so, they began courting and Caroline Twigg was soon to find that Ossie was kind and gentle, and quite a suitable match for her only daughter. They were engaged in 1921 but the sealing of the knot was delayed, not because of any unsuitability but rather because my father was not one to make up his mind quickly. First there was unemployment, but Ossie was rarely out of work as a skilled fitter and turner; then there was Caroline's final illness in 1926; then there was the problem of his mother who could not of course be left. But come September 1929 the question had at last been popped. The newly-weds moved first into his mother's house at 100 Heywood Street and later into the new house at the corner of Heywood Street South and Wellington Road which his mother chose, furnished and decorated to her taste.

It was a semi-detached house, typical of thousands built all over England in the 1930s: well designed, solidly constructed and easily adaptable to future changes of fashion. There were three bedrooms, two of them large and the other a small box-room which was eventually to become mine. Grandma, of course, with first choice, had the front bedroom and my parents the back (albeit with the better view). Downstairs was a long narrow kitchen with a stone sink, gas cooker and large heavy mangle, beside which stood the copper where the clothes were first boiled and possed before being laboriously wound again and again through the rollers of the mangle. I still bear a scar on my forehead from when I tripped on the step from the back yard and fell on the handle of the mangle.

We lived, ate and argued in the back room downstairs, always oppressive with the heat of a huge coal fire and constantly-drying clothes; and in the evening and at weekends, thick with tobacco smoke. Meanwhile the front room was preserved, damp and aseptic, for when we had 'company'. In reality it was rarely used for this as Grandma did not like visitors coming to the house. But the piano was there and my mother, an accomplished pianist, enjoyed an occasional snatched half-hour before Grandma interrupted with a snarled 'We never had time to play pianos or read books when I were your age!' And the pleasure came to its usual abrupt end.

Grandma was born Mary Alice Baldwin in Bury in December 1876. The Baldwins were a large, poor, working-class Victorian family. As well as Mary Alice, there were at least two brothers – Robert and William – and Emily, younger than Mary Alice and with all the endearing qualities her elder sister seemed to lack.

Economic necessity demanded large families of the Victorian poor, and Mary Alice began working amid the terrifying noise of a spinning mill when she was five years old. At first she worked mornings from six o'clock, probably sweeping or picking the cotton refuse from between the looms – a dangerous task which crippled and killed many of these tiny children. By the age of fourteen she was working a full week, driving four looms of her own. The 1870 Education Act had ordained schooling to be

4

available for all, and by 1880 this became compulsory. The Baldwins were sensible enough to want to take advantage of it and some payment was made from the family's meagre income. Basic though it was – schooling in the three Rs rather than true education – the children could and did learn to read and write.

Grandma Austin's brothers William and Robert both fought in the trenches in the First World War and suffered for the rest of their lives from the effects of poison gas. I remember them vaguely as two old men in cloth caps and rough suits who smoked pipes, filling the house with the smell of strong shag and the noise of retching coughs.

Uncle Will lived with us for the last months of his life, and my own first meeting with death – and one of my earliest memories – was when I saw him laid out in his coffin in the front room. I suspect there were long arguments about this, and it was one of the few occasions when my mother won. At the heart of her faith was the fact of Our Lord's bodily resurrection and the certainty of life everlasting. For her, there was nothing to fear in death and a dead body was the empty shell left behind, with no power to hurt. At any rate, I saw the body and – whether for that reason or another – have never had any fear of death or dying.

Grandfather Twigg had one sister, Emma. What Aunt Emma lacked in the piety of her brother, she made up in her quaint eccentricity. She was a delightful Margaret Rutherford-type character who lived in a country cottage halfway up the hill from Jericho to Birtle. Birtle Dean and Ashworth Valley are the local Bury beauty spots, and Aunt Emma's cottage was conveniently placed to receive guests on the way to walks and picnics – my mother, myself and friends, later just myself and friends, occasionally on my own. It was full of delights for small boys and we were always welcomed with drinks, cakes and sweets and homemade apple pie. There was a orchard of apples, plums and crab apples. The cottage, white and spick and span, had brasses and ornaments and trinkets – and of course Aunt Emma. She was a teacher by profession, and even for a year my own class teacher at Fishpool Council Infants' School, so she knew most of my friends by name. We loved her.

Caroline Twigg, my maternal grandmother, was born Payne. Her father was a fisherman in Newlyn and Mousehole in Cornwall, owner of four of five boats, and there are still Paynes in Penzance and Newlyn whom I have never met but who are certainly related to us.

But we are shaped more by those family relationships which are, for good or ill, close and frequent. Family background is part of everyone's story, for the experiences of parents can affect children unto the third and fourth generation. Mine is the story of a journey to faith, not an autobiography. And without a shadow of doubt it was my mother who most shaped the foundations of my Christian faith.

Chapter two

Home, Sweet Home

Two days after my parents had celebrated their silver wedding anniversary in September 1954, my mother was taken ill. I was in my final year at Chichester Theological College and myself happened at that time to be 'in between' medical operations. Surgery to remove a pilonidal sinus had been unsuccessful and I was waiting to return home from the long vacation term to enter Bury General Hospital for a repeat performance. My father was vague about the nature of her illness, and it was only when our next-door neighbour wrote to reassure me that 'there was nothing to worry about' and that she was 'sure Mother was going to be all right', that I began to realise that all was not well.

She had been having headaches and some loss of vision, and the local consultant immediately diagnosed pressure on the brain, probably from a tumour. We went with her as she was transferred, in a nightmarish, bone-shaking ambulance, the eight miles to Salford Royal Infirmary. An emergency operation to relieve the pressure took place and samples were removed for diagnosis. A few days later, we were called in to speak to the consultant, who confirmed that tests had shown the tumour to be malignant and that she had perhaps three weeks to live.

It so happened that the chaplain of Salford Royal at that time was the vicar of St Philip's, Salford, the Reverend Gwilym Morgan, whom I knew well as a former curate at Bury Parish Church. I asked him if my mother could be anointed, and in a quiet ceremony at her hospital bed this was done and she received the Blessed Sacrament. She was in God's hands – and the surgeon's, who explained that he must have permission for a second operation for further relief of pressure. This was agreed, and we waited anxiously for the result. We were told afterwards that the consultant was one of the leading brain surgeons in the country, if not in the world, and when we came into his office we found a very pensive man.

He explained that the second operation had involved drilling two holes in the back of the skull and probing the brain with a knitting-needle-like instrument. 'As I probed,' he said, 'I realised that what I was touching was not the brain but the tumour, and so I have removed it.' He paused, and then continued, 'I should explain that from the x-rays, we knew that the tumour was lodged in the centre of the brain. It had somehow travelled from where it was irremovable to where I found it, and I should have said this was impossible. I am not a Christian believer and I have no explanation as to how this happened. I know what your explanation will be.'

Perhaps in thirty-five years medical science has so advanced that a scientific interpretation is now possible. But that, for me, is irrelevant: either way, God acted in his world and in my mother, in order to give her six more months of life, and the priest who cared for her at our home was to say that those were perhaps the most important spiritually of her whole life.

When she returned home after the second operation, I came up again from Chichester to see her. A bed had been made up in the front room, and as I came in and kissed her, she smiled. 'I'm quite all right, love,' she said. 'I'm not worried and I'm not in much pain. And do you know,' she went on, 'I don't even hate Grandma now.'

I fought back the tears. My sweet, gentle, loving, devout mother had carried this secret deep inside her for so many years. She loved – almost worshipped – my father, and would not have dreamed of hurting him by saying how much she hated his mother. She could not have told me when I was a boy, lest it should nurture the same feelings in me, yet she had no way of knowing that I had no feelings of either love or hatred for the

8

woman who had caused so much pain in our lives. And when I was adult, she would have known that I could not have kept her pain to myself.

Before she married my father, Mother had been a three-times-a-Sunday churchgoer, and involved in choir and other activities at Christian Church Baptists. In a few short years of marriage, this had all gone and I only remember – and that when just a small child – occasional outings to chapel for major festivals such as Harvest, Sermon Sunday, the Sunday school anniversary and the annual church picnic. Who could forget the hymn for the children's collection: 'Hear the pennies dropping, listen as they fall!'?

That my mother ceased regular church attendance was of course a victory for Grandma, who 'didn't go in for that rubbish' and believed that those who did were hypocrites – not understanding that if hypocrites were not welcome in a place where sins are forgiven and grace bestowed then there was little point in having a church at all.

Simply for the sake of peace, my mother gave up the battle. If the price of freedom from a Saturday build-up of tension and a Sunday marred by endless rows was that she should cease to attend church, then the price had to be paid. But she could still pray and read her Bible, and this she did every day of her life. I find incomprehensible the arguments of those who object to asking for the prayers of the saints, for I cannot believe that my mother, who prayed for me constantly in this life, should have ceased to do so when nearer to God in the state of eternal life.

It was of course impossible for my mother to shield her young child from the tensions which were ever-present around Grandma. In any case, her household chores left little time for relaxation and because she was an excellent cook, dressmaker, needlewoman and knitter, some of the chores she could transform into relaxation.

When I was born, Grandma was only fifty-five years old, not ill, not handicapped, not incapacitated in any way. But apart from 'helping to wash the pots', dusting, and occasionally taking

9

me out in my pram or push-chair, I cannot recall that she eased the load from my mother's shoulders in any way. Without the benefits of modern gadgets, my mother scrubbed, polished, cleaned, cooked, for long hours of every day. There were occasional outings to the Co-op shop in Killon Street, with its sawdust-strewn floor, sugar in blue bags, and a sweet/sour mix of smells: fresh bread, turps, cabbages, vinegar, coffee fresh-ground. She never forgot the occasion when one small boy, her back turned, devoured a huge cream cake, with no way of destroying the evidence of his crime.

Every day the milk lady would call. Foot's farm was just a hundred yards away in Wellington Road, a whitewashed stone building lying in a field below the road. They had half a dozen cows at most and somehow eked out a living. One Sunday afternoon, a small crowd gathered as one of the beasts lay prostrate, mooing in agony, with Mr Foot wringing his hands and crying out to all who would hear: 'Oo's deeing on me 'ands!' Every day Mrs Foot would arrive at our front gate in her pony and trap, wooden and highly polished, announcing her arrival at the backdoor with a clank of pail against metal pint ladle and a cry of 'Milk-O!'. It was all completely unhygienic, and I have since wondered if the tuberculosis which was eventually to bring my discharge from the RAF and change the direction of my life did not come from the cows in the Wellington Road field.

As well as daily and weekly duties for my mother, there were special events. About once every six weeks, she would lay a special cloth over the fringed green covering which always graced the dining-room table. The silver dinner service and other wedding presents were taken out of their padded boxes and laboriously cleaned and polished. Then they were put away, never to be used, until their next cleaning. What eventually happened to them I never knew.

Then there was brass to be mirror-polished, much of it around the fireplace: coal-tongs and brush, a poker, the large and elaborate fender with knobs and twirls, and a copper kettle which always rested, warming, on a stand by the fire. Then there was Grandma's display cabinet in the front room, full of dainty crockery, a coffee set too delicate to be used, Victorian ornaments, and highly-coloured wine-glasses etched 'Hare and Hounds Hotel'. There were cut-glass vases, polished but never used, for Grandma would not allow flowers in the house, since they 'attracted flies'. Something certainly did, for there were always sticky, enmeshed insects, feebly struggling and slowly dying on the strips of yellow fly-paper which hung in kitchen and sitting-room.

Monday was washing day, and mother's hands reddened as she spent the day scrubbing dirty clothes and sheets with hard soap and then beating them with a posser, up and down and around in the near-boiling and gradually cooling water of the metal washing-tub, before wringing them out laboriously through the rollers of the heavy mangle. Then they had to be hung out to dry, in the back yard on rare warm, dry days, but most weeks draped over the fireguard and wooden 'maidens', or hanging from the ceiling over and around the sitting-room fire. She could at least have had a washing machine – primitive and old-fashioned by our standards – to relieve the drudgery. But Grandma was adamant: 'I'm not 'aving one o' them dangerous things in my house!' So the drudgery continued.

In the 1930s, the middle classes had maids and we were much lower down that well-defined social scale. But what need had Grandma of a maid when she had my mother: cook, housekeeper, scullery maid, tweeny, daily-woman, footman and butler all rolled into one? Yet my mother never complained, and had she not told me, those years later, that her hatred of Grandma had gone, I should never have known it was there.

If my mother's lot seems hard to modern ears, it was no harder than that of most housewives in the Thirties – less so, for my father's unemployment was in the 1920s, long before marriage. The lines between men's and women's work were clearly defined, and I well remember my father's ridicule on hearing that when I visited a friend's house in my teens I joined with the brothers and sisters there in doing the washing-up. I cannot recall my father ever doing the dishes or even making a cup of tea.

As Tuesday was half-day closing for my father's shop, it became a tradition that my parents had an evening of escapism at the pictures – almost always the Odeon, for Father was a creature of habit. I joined them when I was old enough – from about ten to thirteen, after which small boys did not go to the cinema with their parents, even when it meant being paid for in the dress circle. After all, you might be observed by school friends!

The other landmark of the week was rent night. Every Friday at six o'clock, rain or shine, my mother trudged down Alfred Street and up to Laurel Street to collect the rents at Grandma's houses. It took a couple of hours, and of course she was not paid. When I was old enough, I used to go with her, and I enjoyed hearing the conversations about family crises, faulty drains, leaky roofs and broken downspouts. Could I but have known I would one day be an archdeacon hearing all the same stories about vicarages!

Mother kept many friends from her single days and from the church, but none could call in for tea and a chat, for the price of Grandma's unpleasantness was too great to pay and there was a surfeit of tension and argument as it was. Father came and went, off early in the morning and home late in the evening, often to be greeted by Grandma's newest grievance, usually associated with something I had done – and for which I had to bear the blame, justly or not.

It was only the subconscious awareness that Mother was silently on my side that prevented greater scars. When – as sometimes I did – I screamed insults that I was once again being blamed for what was not my fault, or, alone in my room, cried until I ached at the injustice, or licked my wounds if my father had beaten me, she would squeeze my arm if no one watched or come quietly to my room to cuddle and console me. Always she was loyal to my father and never took my side against him.

Perhaps she ought to have done: but I think he would not have understood.

And of an evening when both Father and Grandma had gone about their separate business, I would sit on her knee, her arms enfolding me, and I knew that love was always there amid the pain. And that itself was the beginning of a knowledge of God.

A measure of freedom for my mother came with the war. About the time I was born, Father had gone into partnership with a cousin, Uncle Tom Byrom, in a wholesale and retail tobacconist shop in Haymarket Street, Bury, since demolished for a town-centre shopping precinct. He loved it and eventually, with Grandma's grudging and oft-trumpeted help, he had bought out his partner and The Shop was his.

It was a thriving concern and he added the franchise of a booking office for Ribble Motors, the local long-distance coach service. He was wholesale supplier of cigarettes and tobacco to a host of small corner shops and pubs in the town, and I earned my first wage delivering the parcels on Saturday mornings. The beneficial side-effect of this was that almost everywhere a small boy could buy his first packet of fags was closed to me. My father would have been told even before the match had been struck! By the time I could have smoked, I had lost the desire.

When the war came Father was thirty-nine years old and by the time conscription caught up with him, he was in his forties. Too old to fight, he was offered a job with the NAAFI – in effect as manager of a shop. He pointed out that he was a trained fitter and turner and suggested he would be more use to the war effort using these skills. By sheer good fortune, he was drafted to work for Ferranti's, who had taken over a cotton mill in Alfred Street, Bury, five minutes' walk from home. He spent most of the war there, making gyroscopes for torpedoes.

But what should be done with the shop? My parents desperately wanted to keep it, and it was agreed that my mother would take over, with my father coming each evening, if possible, to help with the accounts.

13

For Mother it was liberation: a release from bondage into a glorious freedom to be herself. Like many people, she found that, in spite of the fears, bombs, shortages, sadnesses, the war was the happiest time of her life. Tobacco was still included in Atlantic cargoes, and enough escaped the U-boats to sprinkle the empty shelves with occasional supplies as well as keeping the wholesale side of the business active. Mother thrived on it: she loved the work, was calm and friendly with customers and quickly became once again a person in her own right. As a means of eking out the meagre food rations, I would meet her every day for lunch of spam and chips in the UCP restaurant. Without the brooding presence of Grandma, lunch at any rate was without stress. Life as a whole improved for both of us.

There was a partial bonus, too, with holidays. Only on their Bournemouth honeymoon did my parents spend any length of time together without Grandma coming too. I have dim memories of grim holidays in grim boarding houses in Fleetwood, where Grandma would have arguments with fellow-inmates, and where I would be entreated to be 'nice' to her and smacked if my resolve cracked under the strain.

I still recall family shock when, at a seaside concert-party in the Marine Hall, Fleetwood, in August 1939, I laughed uproariously at a rude joke from the stand-up comic: 'Young lady went to the doctor. Doctor said, "Do you know you're going to have a baby?" "Well," she said, "I never did!" He said, "You must have done!" ' ... 'He doesn't know what it means,' declared Grandma. 'Oh yes, he does,' said my mother. And I did. For had we not had our totally inadequate or even non-existent knowledge of sex expanded by a fellow eight-year-old's well-attended, highly exaggerated, often-fantasised lectures on the subject in the playground of St Chad's Junior School?

But on the whole, sex, along with swearing and blasphemy, played little part in my home education. Indeed, when my mother was doing the washing for an ATS girl billeted on our neighbours and I expressed astonishment at a garment I now

14

know to be a size 42 bra, it was whisked out of my sight with the skill of a magician. 'Nothing little boys should know about!' said my mother.

If my parents were silent about sex, at the same time they were sensible. By the time I was thirteen or fourteen, I was of course going to the cinema without my parents. It was some measure of the changing times that whatever the dangers of the war, it was possible for a young boy or girl to be out even in the darkness of the blackout without the fears for their safety that parents today rightly have. When I grew out of the Odeon Saturday morning children's cinema (Buck Rogers, Flash Gordon, Hopalong Cassidy, the Lone Ranger – oh, the joys!), I would occasionally go to a Saturday matinee.

It was then that I discovered the Bury Hippodrome, fifty yards round the corner from my father's shop. It was my first real live theatre and I loved it. Afterwards, I called in at the shop and told my parents (it was Saturday, so both were there) that I would go the next Saturday as well. There was a silence. They looked at each other and said nothing. What I had not realised was that the highlight of the following week's show was nude tableaux, frozen in the Lord Chamberlain's regulations. I never knew what passed between my parents, but they did not forbid me to go. Come the following Saturday afternoon, off I went to the Hippodrome. I was astonished when the nudes appeared, found them mildly interesting but less so than the statues in Bury Art Gallery (where we would take off the fig-leaves to see what was underneath) – and then cringed with embarrassment when I realised that it was the nudes that my parents had assumed I wanted to see. The subject was never mentioned again.

Even so, it was sex, in a sense, which caused a breach in my relationship with my mother. My own son was to grow up in an age with its own problems. But he and his friends – of both sexes – could have relations with each other which were no more than friendships. I did not, and even though for most of us a romantic evening out with a girl in the back row of the cinema meant a kiss and a cuddle and no more, it was not possible for a boy to have a friend who was a girl but not a girlfriend.

My first date ended with a bitter argument with my mother. We had been to the first house, held hands on the back row, exchanged the statutory six or seven chaste kisses. I wanted to ask the girl out again but thought she would say no. So that was that, and I arrived home about eight-thirty. My mother was alone – an ominous sign. 'Where have you been?' 'The pictures.' 'Who with?' 'A friend.' 'What friend?' I was silent.

'You were seen going into the Scala Cinema with a Girl,' said my mother, with *Girl* in a tone which invested the poor lass with all the characteristics of a creature from the Black Lagoon. I felt (and had been) spied upon and went hot with anger. 'Do you have me watched? Who told you?' I shouted. 'I'm not telling you, and don't speak to me like that!' she replied, 'I want to know who she was.' I was silent. 'I'm your mother and I have a right to know.' I was still silent, for I somehow knew that we had reached a watershed. I had done nothing of which I was ashamed to tell my mother, but it was not important or serious enough to tell her about. And above all, I wanted to feel I had some life of my own as an individual – I suppose today one would say, I wanted space to be myself. So I took a deep breath: 'I won't tell you who she was because it's my business and not yours – and no, I'm not ashamed of her. She isn't the first girl I've taken out (a lie) and she won't be the last. If they are serious, I'll tell you, on condition you tell me who told you tonight.' Of course, she could not do that, and as a result I never discussed my love life with my mother – to her great disappointment – and never brought a girlfriend home.

Perhaps it was for the best, given the infinite capacity my family possessed for embarrassing me before my friends. When I was twenty-one, my father reluctantly agreed to have a dinner-dance at the Knowsley Hotel in Bury. Friends from university as well as Bury came, together with a few friends of my parents. After dinner there was a band to lead the dancing and it and the room were booked until midnight. At 10.30 p.m., my father dismissed the band and said it was time for an end. Seeing my face, red with anger and humiliation, my mother said to me quickly, 'Don't spoil the evening!' To my father I said, 'The evening hasn't finished and I'm inviting some of my friends to the house' – which I did. We sat down drinking tea and chatting quietly, while my mother and father went to bed. Well before midnight came the final humiliation: my parents both appeared at the sitting-room door, in pyjamas, dressing gowns and – in my mother's case – curlers. 'We think you'd all better go now – Grandma might come down.' I burned with shame, but felt the kindness and sympathy of my friends as they bade me good night.

My mother had been quietly proud and delighted when I announced that I thought I had a vocation to the priesthood. She had grave doubts about the Church of England and asked me again and again, 'Are you quite sure that Anglicans believe in the bodily resurrection?' In those happier days, I was able without qualification to give her the assurance she asked, but she remained uncertain.

In the end she was convinced, not by argument but by ministry. When she was anointed in hospital I explained to Gwilym Morgan that, though she had deep faith, she was not a member of the Church of England, and to my relief he was happy to give her the sacraments. Later, at home, Fr Leslie Pickett, a good and holy old-fashioned Anglo-Catholic, then Vicar of Holy Trinity, Bury, visited her regularly. She made her first confession, and was confirmed at her bedside by Bishop Frank Woods, the Bishop of Hulme.

She died quietly on Sunday morning, 24th April 1955, exactly six weeks before I was made deacon in Blackburn Cathedral.

It was of course a terrible blow to my father. When we had been given the news of the terminal nature of Mother's illness, we stopped on the way home from Salford for a drink in a Whitefield pub – the first time, I recall thinking, he had ever acknowledged I was old enough to drink (I was then twenty-three). He

17

was sad and thoughtful, and eventually turned to me, tears in his eyes, and said, 'We must be very close now.' And I knew we could not be.

Then he gave me confirmation, if any were needed, that this was so. 'You know,' she said, 'I think what's brought this on in your mother is worrying about you. She was really upset when you had your operation.' I swallowed back the tears, for I knew I could say nothing to him which would not compound the desolation he was feeling. But was this awful happening in our lives to be made more awful by my having to carry the blame? It had been the story of my life and I cannot ever remember it being otherwise.

When Father died in 1975, his friends and acquaintances wrote warm, wonderful letters about 'dear old Ossie': a good friend, always full of fun and ready for a joke, would do anything for anyone, you only had to ask. I knew that all they said was true: he was a good, kind, jolly, warm-hearted, generous man about whom no one could have a bad word to say. I knew too that he loved me dearly and was in his own way proud of me.

I did not need to try to earn his love but I knew I could never have his respect. Never once can I remember him praising me for what I had done: always there was a critical caveat or a suggestion that I had succeeded thanks to the help or influence of others. Never once can I recall him taking my side, and only once not taking the side of another. This was the day of my mother's funeral, when – of all days – Grandma decided in her own inimitable way to start a row, I think about an imagined slight from the nurse whom we had engaged during the last weeks of my mother's life.

We were all tense, and for me this was just too much. I am prone to shouting in arguments, but my family tell me I am at my most dangerous when I am quiet. In a firm, quiet voice I asked Grandma if she couldn't just have left it off for one day. Had she not treated my mother like dirt, I went on, from the day she married my father, made her life miserable? Out it all came, built up over twenty-three years of resentment. Grandma was stunned and for once speechless, and open-mouthed could only look again and again to my father for his usual verbal or physical support. I expected the outburst every moment that I spoke, but this time it never came. All he said was, 'That's enough, Mother.'

When, during my teenage years, the debate began about corporal punishment which could then be ordered by magistrates, my father declared that he had 'always been against corporal punishment'. I laughed ruefully. 'I hadn't noticed!' I said. 'That's different,' was his reply. While he never beat me as hard, for instance, as I was caned by the headmaster at my junior school, I was frequently hit across the face (the last time at the age of seventeen, when he knocked me off a chair), and, if I was thought to have been very naughty, strapped with his leather belt.

The first time I can recall was the day I asked to help with the gardening. Our house stood on a corner plot and consequently had a tiny paved backyard and a large garden at the front and side. My father, who hated gardening almost as much as I do, had laboriously planted bedding plants along the borders of the paths, and had begun to pull out the unsightly chickweed. I announced to my mother that I – still too young for school – would finish the weeding. When my father came home for lunch, I had weeded everything – chickweed, every other weed, together with all my father's bedding plants – and thrown them on the rubbish heap. It was an innocent mistake and I expected praise. I can still see my father coming through the gate from the back yard, pulling the belt from his trousers. I was carried upstairs, thrown on the bed, and my screams were as much at the injustice of it as at the pain.

My childhood memories merge into a constant row, but of course it was not really so. But there were indeed many rows, for although I learned to curb my anger, there were times when I could stand Grandma's taunts and criticisms no longer and would burst out with a torrent of abuse, all the more violent for its earlier repression. One winter's evening, late home from school, I was eating my tea alone. Grandma 'started' on me and eventually, still under control but only just, I shouted at her, 'Please will you for once – *just* – *leave* – *me* – *ALONE!*' That, of course, was enough to make her redouble her complaints. I made the supreme sacrifice – my largely uneaten meal: I threw the remains of my first course at her, plate and all, followed by several sticky rounds of toast and strawberry jam, and then the large text-book from which I was doing my homework.

Of course, sometimes it was I who was at fault, sometimes half of one and half of the other, and sometimes simply Grandma. 'Wait till your father gets home!' she would threaten. I knew that, when he did, for the sake of peace it would be my fault. And it always was.

My father tried hard to make a relationship between us and as a small child he would tease me. He was a great practical joker – he and Uncle Tom at the shop had more than once put a luckless lad, mistaking the tobacconist's for the next door barber's, into a chair with a sheet around him. When I took it as a fatherly invitation to reciprocate, that was a different matter.

Football brought us as close as anything ever did, though initially it was a cause of yet more pain. At the Junior School, I was chosen for the school team and set out proudly in my new strip. No one had taught me what to do or even how to kick a ball but I enjoyed myself on Wellington Road playing fields. When I came home, delirious at victory, my father told my mother that he had watched for a time, unseen by me. I think he hoped I might follow – as he had never been good enough to do – in his own father's footsteps, and play at least semi-professionally. 'How did he get on?' my mother asked. He looked at me and laughed. 'He'll never make a footballer!' I was an over-sensitive child just as I am probably an over-sensitive adult. The balloon was punctured and never re-inflated.

But my father was an avid fan of Bury Football Club and looked forward to the day when his only son would join him. There was a Boys' Stand in those days and he bought me a season ticket. All I remember is that the first match was against Liverpool and that I actually saw in the flesh a player, Niewenhuys, whose image I had on a cigarette card.

After the war, I had a season ticket for many years, now old enough to join my father and his cronies at first in the enclosure, and later, when he became a director and eventually vice-chairman of the club, in the director's box. He was somehow at home in the world of football and it was only on those occasions that he seemed able to see me as an adult and almost as an equal. When I was a curate in London, I would arrange to have time off on those Saturdays when Bury were playing in the area. We would meet for lunch and travel in the team coach to the ground, and it was the nearest we came to friendship. And it was not confined to Bury Football Club.

A fellow-member of Christian Church Cricket Club in Bury was Joe Shaw, full-back in the great Arsenal team of the 1930s, and he and my father became great friends. Known as Gentleman Joe as a player, Joe Shaw was not only a great footballer and later chief coach with Arsenal for many years. He was the kindest of men and a devout Christian – and with a natural rapport with keen young football fans like Ossie's son, George. When I was a student at Chichester, he was still serving the club and on rare occasions I would be able to travel up for matches, when he was a gracious, attentive and kindly host.

Joe would always provide a couple of tickets for the Cup Final so that, even before my father had his own supply as a director at Bury, he and I would travel every April to Wembly – as he had done from the very first Wembley Final – when no expense was spared. He spent little on entertainment and almost nothing on holidays but this was his annual extravagance: first class travel, sleepers (in the days when a fast train from Manchester to London took four-and-a-half hours), often a couple of nights at a good hotel. My first final was in 1946 – Charlton against Derby County – and, with the exception of perhaps the greatest, the Matthews final between Blackpool and Bolton Wanderers in

1953 when I was sitting my university finals, we were there I think for twenty-two consecutive years, with a sprinkling later.

My decision to be ordained was a grave disappointment to my father, for his dearest wish had been that I should join him in the shop. When I worked there for a time during a university long vacation, I believe he really felt the experience might persuade me to 'pack it all up' there and then. If so, it was a disaster.

What he saw as a gentle fatherly tease had over the years developed into a tendency to humiliate. He seemed to resent – I think quite unconsciously – the fact that I was at university, and he would never talk about it or ask me what it was like. Again and again when I served a customer, the customer, with that curious Bury rudeness, would discuss me with my father as if I were not there. 'I see you've got him working, Ossie.' 'Aye – these students don't know what work is. Eight weeks idleness and then three months holiday to get over it.' 'He wants to do some real work.' 'Ee, no, by heck! I think it 'ud kill him!'

I have long had the ability to put down with a nasty quip, and it is an unkind gift I have to curb. For the most part I let the matter ride, tight-lipped and red with anger. Just occasionally, I snapped back – in the nicest way, of course – with a comment that might not have been taken for what it was intended. 'You can't take a joke,' my father would say angrily. 'I really don't know where you'll end up.' And he just could not understand why I left and found a different vacation job.

After I was ordained, his lack of confidence in me began to take on ludicrous proportions. When, unhappy in my first curacy, I left at the earliest date open to me, I found that in my father's eyes alone I had left under a cloud. When a later job, with the London University chaplaincy, came to a premature end, he automatically assumed that I had been lazy/incompetent/above myself/a total failure as expected. It was impossible to discuss the matter with him. 'You really will have to try in your next job,' he told me seriously, 'or you might as well pack it in.' He was quite unable to appreciate that his son was not twelve but twenty-nine, and perfectly able to look after himself in a world totally alien to his father's experience.

Perhaps the most ludicrous misunderstanding was when the Bishop of St Albans offered me my first incumbency, at St Mary the Virgin, Eaton Bray. At the time, I had a slight acquaintance with a local football worthy, Bert England, whom my father knew from his own world of club directors.

On the day of my induction, my father commented knowledgeably, 'You know, you've Bert England to thank for this.' 'For what?' I asked. 'Becoming Vicar of Eaton Bray,' he replied. I was silent for a moment, puzzled. 'Whatever do you mean?' I asked. Nodding sagely he answered, 'He'll have pulled a few strings for you to get it.' Even he, I thought, cannot be serious. 'Don't be silly!' I said and laughed. It was, I fear, the laughter that was the mistake. He boiled with anger: 'You don't know how these things work. With your record, you needed a bit of help and Bert thinks a lot of you.' There was no point in arguing: he could not conceive that the Bishop might also think enough of me to make the appointment. I went over to the church for the induction service, soured and saddened, aware that my father could not bring himself to believe in his own son.

I know that I am prickly and abrasive, with a short fuse, likely to explode more quickly than some, if less so now than in my youth. Why then did I almost never take my father to task? Almost never? Only once, in fact.

Years later, he had come to stay with us at Bushey Heath with my stepmother (he married an old family friend, Ellen Loy, in 1959) and two friends from Bury. As a parent will (and as I do with my long-suffering son) stories of 'I remember when you were a little boy' began yet again to be related. And he told a favourite story of how, when I was about eight years old I had bought them all Christmas presents: two candles for my father, a box of matches for my mother and a mousetrap (something Freudian there, I wouldn't doubt!) for Grandma. Did I remember? he asked.

Indeed, I did, I replied, carrying on the story with a fixed smile. I explained that it had been the first time I had been old enough to buy presents on my own with pocket money I had saved. I had spent hours walking round Bury market until I had made my choice. 'And you ridiculed me to all the neighbours and humiliated me before my friends. Everyone who came was told and was encouraged to laugh at this great joke. That's why you got a tie every year after that.' There was an embarrassed silence around the table. My father hung his head and I thought he would cry. 'I never knew,' he said quietly. And I bitterly regretted I had reacted as I had. Why did I never take him to task? It could only be because, whatever my resentment, I loved him and could not hurt him.

And there was resentment: resentment that I was always in the wrong, always the cause of every ill that beset the family; resentment that he could never praise me if I succeeded; resentment that not only could he not treat me as an adult but that he seemed unable to grant me any rights or distinctiveness as an individual. One incident sums up this latter attitude.

I had owned and treasured a nine-volume *Times* history of the First World War. They were newspaper-size and therefore both bulky and heavy, and rather than take them from parish to parish while I was an assistant curate and risk damage or loss, I had asked if I could leave them at home with him. I used to stay there for my holiday break after major festivals, and one Christmas, just before I returned, he said, 'Oh, by the way, you know those big books about the War you left here? I've given them to East Ward School.' He was by then on the Bury Education Committee and governor of a number of schools.

'What do you mean, you've "given them to East Ward School"?' I asked. 'They don't belong to you to give to anyone. I left them here for you to look after for me.' A look, both pained and angry, filled his fate: 'But I didn't think you'd mind. The headmaster was very pleased to have them.' I took a deep breath and tried to explain: 'But they weren't your property. Didn't you even think to ask me?' 'I don't need to ask. We're family: it's not "mine" and "yours" but "ours".' 'You mean if I took that picture off the wall and gave it to someone, I could do?' 'Now you're just being silly. That was a wedding present.' 'Well, you'll just have to see the head at East Ward and get them back.' That was a humiliation he could not face. 'I can't do that,' he said in a hurt voice. My stepmother joined the fray: 'You've upset your father.' I gave up, for I knew he could never understand, not simply that he had given away something he did not own, but more important that his son was an individual in his own right.

But resentment never overcame my love for him, and I sometimes pondered why this should be. In the end it was my stepmother, some years after his death, who unwittingly provided the clue. We were visiting her soon after the publication of the fateful *Crockford's* Preface and the suicide of its author, Canon Gareth Bennett. I had been suggested as one who might have been its author and for three weeks, before and after the tragic events, had been chased by reporters from the national media.

My stepmother had 'caught' my father's attitude to me, and when the media began to call me while my wife and I were staying with her, she immediately assumed that I was not only in waters too deep for me, but naturally at fault as well – and mistakenly said so. Unfortunately by that time I had interred any resentment I might have had towards my father and her comments had the effect of exhuming them. But they also had a beneficial result.

I explained to my stepmother, as gently as I could, that she could have no conception of the matters under discussion, nor of their importance for the church, nor of my place and involvement in them. But nor had she the right to assume that I must naturally be in the wrong. My father was allowed to do that because he was my father, but she could not. The implications of what I was saying I realised only afterwards: that a relationship of love can accept anything – hurts, injustices, humiliations, rejections. I must have loved my father much more than I imagined.

But Grandma I did not. She died in 1958, friendless, with few acquaintances, the only callers one or two indomitable neighbours prepared to bear the whips and scorns of her tongue with true Christian fortitude. Even my father was to say, 'You know, I could never understand why my father drank so much, but the last three years alone with Grandma have made me much more sympathetic to him.'

She was a strange and sad figure, and as a small boy I was convinced that she was a witch. My mother would always take her a large mug of tea in bed, and when it was empty she would use it as the dustbin for the detritus of the night: hair from her brush, nail clippings, used corn-plasters, 'eye of newt and toe of frog, wool of bat and tongue of dog'. It was wiser not to look. Once I was dispatched to 'bring Grandma's cup down' and I entered her bedroom just as she was pouring the unspeakable contents of one mug into another. I viewed her with awe, for I was certain I had caught her just as she changed from whatever shape her witchery took.

She had words which were her own, and it was many years before I realised that when she said (usually about me), 'He's got no discí-pline' – meaning badly behaved – that it was the same word as 'discipline' with the emphasis on the first instead of the second syllable. 'Nast' was what a dog left on the pavement, but it could be used in a variety of contexts. 'Nowt' probably had its origin in 'naughty' but with her, 'He's reet nowt' (usually me again) meant 'He's always answering back.'

Her most curious use was that of the word 'paysegg'. It must have derived from 'pace-egg', with the verbal 'pace-egging' coming from the practice of rolling Easter ('Pasch') eggs down a convenient hill on Good Friday. But with Grandma, 'to paysegg' meant 'to act to the irritation of others'. 'Stop paysegging', she would say to me, and I knew I had yet again left undone those things which I ought have done or done those things I ought not have done.

Yet my very earliest memories always feature Grandma: asking her who all those men were – I can see them now, shabby suits, cloth caps and clogs – in a long line and being told they were queuing for dole money; or waiting at the corner of Knowsley Street and Manchester Road by the statue of the soldier (who for some unknown purpose was apparently holding a bucket above his head) and watching King George V and Queen Mary drive by in a open Daimler on their Silver Jubilee.

A favourite walk was to the engine sheds at Buckley Wells where I could climb on the bars of the level crossing to see the electric trains to Manchester clatter by. But it was the little saddle-tanked steam engines which were the real interest for a small boy, and I can still smell the smoke and the scent of the coal. Coal was everywhere: in heaps to feed the engines but trampled too into the dirt road where the public walked. It was soon all over me, and there was a price to pay. For as soon as a smut settled on my face out would come Grandma's handkerchief. Spitting liberally upon it she would 'clean' my face, and all the way home I would think I could smell its odour and hold my face taut until I could dowse it under the tap.

But the abiding memory is of rows. A real good row Grandma could maintain for several days, as it gradually lost strength like a dying hurricane. It could be there when we went to bed and when we rose the next day; it would continue through breakfast, be there again at lunchtime and renewed in strength over supper, nourished by a day simmering in her self-induced loneliness. As I have said, it was always I who was to be blamed, but I suspect that the longer she made it last, the more it really was my fault.

The most enduring row was certainly my fault. On a sunny August Bank Holiday we had joined the crowds going to Holcombe Hill, a local beauty spot. We caught the train to Holcombe Brook village and climbed halfway up the hill where lived one of Grandma's distant half-cousins three times removed. It was a tiny cottage with oil lamps and an outside toilet. During tea, I asked if I could 'go', and was fascinated by the deep hole disappearing into the foetid darkness beneath the wooden seat.

Grandma had decided she too wanted to go, and as I came out there she was. She went in and closed the door. Then I noticed it could be bolted from the outside – and without a moment's hesitation I locked her in. It was a boyish prank, though with more than a little malice behind it.

I returned quietly to my cup of tea and egg sandwiches, with a look of innocence on my face. After about ten or fifteen minutes, there was a break in the conversation and my mother said, 'I wonder where Grandma's got to.' 'I saw her go into the lavatory,' I offered helpfully. A few more minutes passed, and it was decided to send out a search party. She was soon found, for the noise of her angry banging on the wooden door of the privy was heard immediately everyone had left the thick-walled cottage.

However thick, the walls shook as she vented her fury against me. 'He wasn't just paysegging – he might have killed me.' she shrieked. Although I was beaten, it somehow seemed worth it, and I smirked contentedly as I thought of what I had done. But we had it all the way down the hill to the station; the other passengers heard all about it as we were left with space on the crowded platform, and as she rehearsed it over and over again on the short journey back to Bury. It took at least ten days before it eventually petered out, and forever after she would resurrect it if the opportunity came: 'What's more,' she would cry, and the needle would drop into its familiar groove, 'I'll never forget the day he locked me in the lavatory. He wouldn't have cared if I'd died.'

In the early years of the war, leukaemia was diagnosed and Grandma was given three to six months to live. However, it seemed that the Lord was not ready for her – and who could blame Him? In the event there was some kind of remission of the leukaemia and she recovered sufficiently to enjoy her usual malaise, duodenal ulcers. On one of her stays in hospital, I had evidently (at about fourteen years of age) became aware of girls and must have eyed one of the pretty nurses. 'Your grandson has wicked eyes,' she said later to Grandma. On our next visit, Grandma greeted us with an air of triumphant malevolence: 'The nurse says he's got wicked eyes. They're trained, you know, these nurses. She could see straight away what a bad 'un he is. He'll come to a bad end, you mark my words. They know, these nurses, you can't get away from that.'

But it was because of the war that I gained yet another remission from Grandma. It was my father's habit every Friday night to go up to the Crown Inn in Spring Street for a drink with his friends. One of them was Teddy Fletcher, who lived in Price Street, not ten minutes from our home. The day came, early in the war, that my mother, with Grandma eyeing me balefully, asked, 'Would you like to go to the Fletchers' for dinner and tea on Saturday?' I was suspicious and not too enthusiastic. But I could see there was no point in arguing and so I reluctantly agreed to go, just for that Saturday. Injunctions to be on what was fondly called my 'best behaviour' did nothing to dispel my gloomy apprehension. I had hardly been in their house ten minutes before I realised that my doubts were entirely unfounded. Doris and Teddy Fletcher became like second parents to me (though it was years before I called them by their Christian names – even 'Uncle Teddy' and 'Auntie Doris' would have aroused strong disapproval at home).

Doris and Teddy had no children of their own but both had the rare gift of immediate communication with the young. Saturdays quickly fell into a regular pattern, and I would often call on other days as well, sometimes with friends who were greeted with the same warmth and welcome as I was myself. On Saturday afternoons, Teddy and I would go for long walks, so that a boy born and brought up in a town learned a love and respect – and a wonder – for the countryside. Teddy taught me where to find nests of blackbirds and thrushes in the hedgerows, to creep up to a lapwing's nest in a field, to ignore the deception of a skylark trying to lead an intruder away. The song of birds became familiar and I learnt to recognise (but never to touch) the eggs of nesting birds. Once we found a woodcock on its nest and watched its darting flight as if to spoil the aim of its hunters.

Teddy delighted at my own delight and we chattered together as friends. Only one subject was taboo: the war. Teddy had been in the trenches on the western front for most of the First World War and could never bring himself to talk about the experience. Sometimes we would go to the cotton mill where he worked and he would show me the vast engine which was his responsibility and the machinery which depended on it. We would return exhausted and ready for the spam and chips and home-made cakes Doris had prepared for us.

Teddy and Doris made me feel at home, yet at home in a home without rows and ever-present tensions, where I was allowed to be myself without criticism and without the constant feeling that if I was not at fault that moment, then I soon would be. They brought light and happiness into my boyhood years, and I owe them more than I realised at the time. To introduce me to them was a stroke of genius, I suspect on my mother's part. Perhaps she sought to shield me from the same hatred for Grandma that she herself felt.

But in fact I never hated Grandma, in spite of all the unhappiness she brought to our home life. Nor did I have any feelings of love or affection for her – indeed, to be truthful, no more feelings than I would have had for a rather disagreeable stranger at a first meeting. Yet she did have a part to play in the combination of family influences which brought me to the faith I needed in the personal pilgrimage God had prepared for me.

From my mother came the knowledge that love means there is someone there in troubles who cares and supports, and if God is love he is like that. Because of the way my father was, I came to see that love survives hurts and indignities and misunderstandings, and if God is love he is like that. From my father too I gained another important trait. Because I knew I could never gain his praise, I have never sought to succeed in human terms. I have been able to hold to the integrity of my views without compromise, however unpopular they may have been. Never did I feel the need to jockey for the approval that would lead to preferment by following the well-trodden path that so many ambitious modern Vicars of Bray took in the late Seventies and early Eighties. And never once, praise God, did I feel a trace of envy as again and again the willing conformity of the mediocre received its episcopal or decanal or archidiaconal reward. So it should be, for God expects of the Christian, and especially of the Christian priest, not that he should be successful but that he should be faithful. If when I die it can be said of me that I was faithful, I shall ask for no other obituary.

But what did I learn from Grandma? Surely the hard lesson that sometimes I must bite my tongue and not speak out if an injustice is towards me rather than against another; that because one is paranoid, it does not mean one is not persecuted; that verbal abuse need not lead to hatred.

I have never borne personal insults and the like with equanimity and never found the injunction to turn the other cheek an easy one to follow. Indeed it took an incident which must wait the telling until the story has covered another forty years for me to learn the grace to accept that we really are blessed when men revile us and speak evil of us unjustly for the Lord's sake. There have been many occasions in my life when fellow church members have reviled me or spoken evil of me unjustly, and I have reacted quite wrongly in anger and bitterness.

But at least, thanks to Grandma perhaps, if they have produced in me cold indifference, they have never elicited my hatred.

Chapter three

Schooldays

Can anyone not remember the first day at school? I went, in some fear and trepidation, knowing no one. I had played with Peter Jackson and his younger sister Pat, our next-door-but-one neighbours, whose father Harold Jackson had a crockery shop in Haymarket Street near my father's. But they were Catholics. I never quite knew why, but being a Catholic was something one didn't do, like swearing or getting drunk or smoking below the age of thirty-five. But I did notice that they went to church as a family, Sunday by Sunday, and that made its impression on me. Anyway, it meant of course that the children went to a Catholic school, Peter to St Marie's and Pat to the Convent.

So off I went on that first day, holding my mother's hand, probably crying, into the dark unknown. Fishpool Council Infants School was in 1936 only a year or two old. Its quadrangle playground was ideal for a lonely boy to create an imaginary railway track, and I spent playtime chuff-chuffing around on my own.

On Day Two, I was sent to Miss Law, the headmistress, for misbehaving. We had been given coloured chalks for drawing, and I had discovered that I could make a pleasant pattern on the back of the girl sitting in front of me. 'Please miss, that boy's drawn on my coat.'

There are two types of reception class teachers: those who can keep order gently with hardly ever a raised voice and those who shriek without a break from nine in the morning until three-fifteen in the afternoon. My memory of Miss Haslam is that she fell firmly into the latter category. 'Come out here,

George Austin!' she bellowed. And off I went to the head, a tall, formidable lady with dressed almost to her ankles, and grey hair piled on the top of her head, who looked and sounded rather like Queen Mary.

The humiliation was compounded by the knowledge that my parents would be told as soon as school had ended; for we lived next door to the teacher from the top class, Miss Vera Chatterley, and I was aware that my progress was being carefully monitored. There was a post-mortem on the events of that day and my wickedness was savoured and served up as a delicious extra over tea, the main meal of the northern day. Grandma was triumphant: 'I've allus said he were a bad 'un.' And she had.

But Miss Chatterley also provided further and more mysterious information about me: 'He won't be sat on.' I could not understand what she could mean. No one had tried to sit on me, either in the classroom or in the playground. But I was content to be baffled, for whatever it was that had happened, it was in my favour.

At seven we moved up to the older church school next door, St Chad's. It is hard to believe that the glamorous young teacher, Miss Temple, must – if she is still alive – be now well over seventy. Fred Hill, the stern headmaster who once caned me for tickling the boy next to me as we stood in line to march into school, is dead, as is Miss Fogg from the top class. The senior master, Mr Rigby, used a wooden pointer at the blackboard and this doubled as a weapon to be used across the knuckles. When I was a burly six-foot twenty-year-old, I was introduced to a man I towered over. 'Do you know Mr. Rigby?' 'Indeed I do: you used to hit me with a wooden stick.'

St Chad's was a church school in the parish of St Peter's Bury. The vicar and curate came in occasionally to take classes and I can recall the curate rebuking me for saying I went to Christian Church: 'We all go to a Christian Church.' In fact I went only to festivals and it was a new experience to attend St Peter's with the school for a weekday school service. I asked my parents if I might go on a Sunday, so I clearly had enjoyed it. Unfortunately, on Sunday morning it must have been (as I realised years later) Mattins and Litany, and once only was quite enough. Eventually I began to attend Parkhills Methodist Church, where I used to wait outside until I thought the 'long prayer' had finished. Apart from one old lady in a black hat and long black coat, no one was very friendly, so that attendance quickly ended.

Then came the war. I sat on my mother's knee listening to the radio at 11 a.m. on 3rd September 1939 to hear the sad voice of Prime Minister Neville Chamberlain telling the nation that we were at war. My mother cried and said a lot of people would be killed, so I cried too without understanding.

Of course, to a small boy, war was exciting. We were issued with gas masks and had to carry them everywhere. At school we had air-raid practice and learned to squat under desks before outside shelters were built.

In the winter and spring of 1941, during the Manchester blitz, I was studying for the entrance examination to the High School. Night after night, we were roused by the sirens and my father would go out on his duties as an ARP warden, with steel helmet and gas mask. Grandma sat in her bonnet and dressing-gown under the stairs (said to be the safest place), while my mother and I crouched beneath the dining room table. Even though we could hear bombs and anti-aircraft fire, I had no thought that we might be killed, and happily identified the various sounds, distinguishing between the deep throb-throb of German bombers and the lighter roar of our fighters. Some time during that winter, a shelter was dug in the Chatterleys' garden and we slept in bunks there for weeks on end. The smell of damp blankets mingled with the paraffin of the heater and lamp, and old Mr Chatterley insisted on sitting up all night with his hand over the latch-hole of the door, 'so them Germans won't see t'light'.

Shrapnel to be gathered after a raid, anti-aircraft guns pointing skywards near the school, the occasional sight of a Spitfire or a Wellington bomber, or even on one joyous occasion the glimpse of a Nazi Dornier 'Flying Pencil' through a break in the clouds when on the way to school, bombed houses, the town full of American GIs (and sometimes even seeing a younger teacher arm-in-arm with one of them) – it was all a delight to a young lad.

My father disliked the Americans almost as much as he disliked the Germans – and the French, the Poles, the Czechs, the Welsh, the southern English, but most of all the Americans. My mother would have none of it: when I rejoiced at the number of German planes destroyed daily in the Battle of Britain, she would bring me down to earth with a gentle reminder that a German wife or mother would be mourning a dead husband or son. She did not believe that the 'only good German was a dead one', and the lesson went home with me.

By September 1941, not all the younger male teachers had been called up to serve in the forces, but gradually they disappeared one by one – Mr Briant, Mr Rumble, Mr Dodman – to be replaced by the good, the bad and the totally incompetent. The older members of staff held the fort – teachers like Mr Hayward, Miss Sharp, Miss Beech, old Mr Barnes with his gown greened from age, Mr Aisbitt (physics) who took up his dining-room floor to grow mushrooms for the war effort and marshalled us boys to dig up the school garden to raise vegetables, Mr Murden (maths) the most strict and most respected of all, Mr Bunting (chemistry) who ran the stamp club.

Physical education teachers were the first to go, and this had an unexpected and beneficial effect on our social skills. For we were taught ballroom dancing. No generation can have been as expert as ours in the finer arts of quickstep, foxtrot, waltz, military two-step, tango, and the like, and in later teenage years we were to make the most of the boy-meets-girl opportunities the dance-floor provided.

But our general academic education inevitably suffered as the number of good teachers, especially for the younger age-groups, was reduced, and even the return of the permanent staff after

1945 hardly made up, in spite of valiant efforts, for the deprivations of earlier years.

I had the added disadvantage of being eighteen months younger than the average age of my class, so that I was sitting School Certificate (the 'O level' of the day) at only fourteen, too young not to have been bored by the poor standard of so many of the replacement teachers. 'He must bestir himself and make a livelier effort', wrote Mr Woods, the headmaster, on one of my reports, matching the acid comments against too many of my subject marks. Even so, I managed six passes, which was enough for me to continue into the sixth form.

At the High School, I was almost nauseatingly well-behaved. Never in trouble, my Grandmother was wont to comment – in disgust that I avoided the just reward for what she was sure were my misdeeds – 'He must leave his fiddle behind t'door when he goes to school.'

I became a Flight Sergeant in the Air Training Corps, house captain, and in 1948 – to my surprise – school captain. 'Dippy' Briant, the head of English, had returned from war service in the RAF and determined to develop a love of literature in his ignorant charges. What happened for me was that school drama, together with school visits to the theatre, began a love affair with the theatre which has never left me. Donald Wolfit may have been a ham of the highest degree, but his portrayal of King Lear at the Manchester Opera House fulfilled Dippy Briant's desire to bring the better things of culture to at any rate one of his charges.

With the sixth form came the need to decide on a career. It was not difficult: service in the Air Training Corps from the age of fourteen had left me in no doubt that I wanted to be a pilot in the Royal Air Force. I had taken my first flight in an RAF Anson bomber in 1946 – from Salmesbury airfield near Blackburn out to Blackpool, round the tower and back again. I was thrilled – as I still am after hundreds of flights in many parts of the world. So I would join the RAF, not just as a National Serviceman for the statutory two years but as a career. It was not to be.

I was called up on Monday 19th September 1949, and arrived at RAF Padgate for my basic training. In the first week I was subjected to tests of all kinds, including more stringent medicals than those before call-up. On the Wednesday afternoon, I was dispatched from my hut for a further chest x-ray and on the Thursday for an interview with the medical officer. Had I had chest trouble? Only the usual coughs and colds. Were they sometimes very heavy? I did cough up a good deal. Ever coughed up blood? No, never. 'Well, it seems from your x-ray that you've had tuberculosis. It appears to be dormant but we'll want to look at you every three months or so.' I asked if that meant I could not be a flier and explained that I had planned to sign on and make the RAF my career.

There was a whispered consultation between senior and junior doctors. 'In that case, I think we had better grant you a medical discharge.' I suspect that the truth of the matter was that they had decided to treat me as a volunteer rather than as a conscript, and were allowing me to get on with my life without the interruption of National Service.

'What will you do now?' asked the MO. The answer to that was easy. 'I shall go into the church.' The MO looked at me rather anxiously, wondering if there was some psychological disorder in addition to the tuberculosis. 'Don't do anything too hasty,' he cautioned me.

It was 4.30 p.m. on Thursday 22nd September 1949.

Chapter four

Religion and All That

I once said, with all the unfair cleverness of the student, that my mother believed in God and adult baptism, my father in God and the British Empire and my grandmother in God and fortune tellers. But it did have a grain of truth: Grandma was occasionally visited by strange, wizened old ladies, smelling of moth-balls and brandy, with whom she was not to be disturbed while having tea. They would read her palm, her cards and, tea consumed, her tea-leaves as well. She would emerge with a self-satisfied smirk, a half-crown would pass between them, and the old woman would disappear with a promise to return.

When the prophesies were gradually allowed to unfold, the pattern was always the same: good was to happen to Grandma, evil in varying degrees to family, friends and neighbours, and unassailable proof yet again revealed that I was a 'bad 'un'. It was all fairly harmless and as it put Grandma into what with her passed for a reasonably good humour for several days afterwards, it was quite worth while.

Some time during my early childhood, my father began to attend St Paul's Church in Bury, not far from Christian Church Baptists which had been my mother's chapel. The vicar was a formidable, deep-voiced clergyman, Canon Burnell, a preacher of some note in the town. My father came to admire him greatly and as well as attending Mattins or Communion occasionally on a Sunday he also, I believe, belonged to the canon's successful Men's Class.

I was never pressed to join him and meandered for a time happily between St Peter's and Parkhills Methodist until I discovered Bank Street Unitarians. It had an excellent social life, and I found friends from school there. There were prizes for attendance, and for three successive years I gained the special prize given to those who did not miss a single Sunday, morning or afternoon, for a whole year. I cannot recall one single item of religious teaching I culled from all those attendances. But I did become moderately proficient at billiards and snooker.

Bank Street also gave me my first holiday away from my parents. At Great Hucklow in the Derbyshire Peak District, the Unitarian Church had a holiday home and every year, in company with Chesham Unitarians, off we went, first to Manchester and then from Manchester Central on the old London St Pancras line to Millers Dale station. It was more than adventure: during the war there were no taxis in such outlying places and we could not have afforded the fare anyway. So we walked, through Tideswell and on to Great Hucklow, suitcases and all. It was worth it, and after a week we returned, dirty, dishevelled and totally exhausted.

But it also gave me an experience which puzzled me much afterwards. One day we walked back to Tideswell where, for want of anything better to do, we went into the parish church, the 'Cathedral of the Peak'. We were not vandals, for in those days small boys did not vandalise churches. But we did go into the chancel where there was a small harmonium and those who could play the piano began beating out the pop music of the day. I found that I did not like this and refused to join in ('He's soft!') but could not explain why. But it did seem to me that this building – and especially the chancel – was a holy place, and we should not make fun of its sanctity.

But there was nothing of the holy at Bank Street and soon afterwards, at about the age of fourteen or fifteen, I ceased to attend. After that, I went nowhere for a couple of years, though one event put the Christian religion more firmly into my life.

In those days, the Student Christian Movement – before it centred on left-wing political theory – had a division called SCM in Schools. A sixth-form conference was held at Bury Grammar School – I think during April 1948 – conducted probably by the two northern secretaries, John Trillo and John Gibbs. Both were to become bishops, of Chelmsford and Coventry, and in fact John Trillo was first at Bedford and Hertford and a good friend to my family. He baptised our son in 1969. I have no recollection of anything which was said at the Conference but I know that it was the point at which I first began to take the Christian faith with any seriousness.

However, it was not until the Harvest Festival later that year that I astonished my father by saying I was going to join him for Evensong at St Paul's. Canon Burnell has by then moved to be vicar of Dunster in Somerset, but his successor and former curate, the Reverend Dennis Eastwood, had invited him as visiting preacher for the Festival. I can even remember his text: 'We are able', from St John's Gospel.

But it was not religious fervour which drew me. I had recently discovered that a group of girls from school, all of whom seemed to me to be extremely pretty, were regular members of the congregation. Although it proved to be of no help whatsoever to my love life, I began to be 'involved'. The day after the Harvest, I was visited by curate and vicar successively (I was later to discover that it was Mr Eastwood's policy to give his curate a list of visits and then do them all himself as well). I was enrolled into a confirmation class and quickly discovered that one did not need to be a hypocrite to recite the Apostles' Creed, which had formerly been for me a stumbling-block to becoming a member of the Church of England. In fact I found on the contrary that its clauses were perfectly credible, and if in the years that have followed I have had cause to examine them again in the light of critical scholarship, I have never had cause to doubt their veracity.

I have never in my life doubted the existence of God and since becoming an Anglican have never had any doubts about the traditional doctrines which are the church's foundation. I do not say that with any pride, for I know that it means I can be of little help to those Christians who do have doubts. I cannot of course claim to understand how God was incarnate in Jesus Christ, how Christ was born of a virgin mother, how on the third day he rose bodily from the dead, but he ascended to the Father, how he performed miracles during his ministry, how he comes to me in the bread and wine of the Holy Eucharist so that I am filled with all the fullness of the living God. But I know with absolute certainty that all this is so and never for a moment have I doubted it. God, we are told, never tests us above that which we are able to bear, and I can only assume that it is because of a weakness in me that he has shielded me from the doubts and uncertainties that most others have to endure.

I was confirmed by the Bishop of Manchester, Dr William Greer, in Walshaw Parish Church on 30th March 1949. I rather expected to feel the Holy Spirit coming upon me but was of course disappointed. Nor was I aware of any increase in wisdom or understanding or indeed of any other of the seven-fold gifts of the Spirit. I refused to allow my parents to attend, for it was, I felt, something quite private between me and God. They were hurt and did not understand my attitude. I do not think I do now, either.

I attended Mattins and Evensong every Sunday and, under the rule suggested by the vicar, took communion once a month without fail, always fasting. It was about twenty minutes' walk from Parkhills Road to St Paul's, and after the double journey and a half-hour service I was sometimes quite faint. It would have been much simpler to have gone to the 8 a.m. communion at Holy Trinity Church, two minutes' walk from home, but I had somehow been instinctively aware that Holy Trinity was Not Very Nice. It was bad enough to be catholic, but to be Anglo-catholic – well, I suspect that if I had put half the girls in the upper fifth in the family way it would have been received with less disapproval than if I had begun to worship at Holy Trinity. I did, however, begin to divide my time between St Paul's and Bury parish church, where most of my friends from the sixth form worshipped.

In those days the parish church had one of the finest choirs in the country and I began to realise the importance of music for me in worship. And there was a good social life, thanks to the efforts of the curates, Geoffrey Williams and Gwilym Morgan. Geoffrey was to become one of my closest friends and we are godfather to each other's sons, but in those more formal days he was 'Mr Williams' to one and all. During his ten-year curacy at Bury, Mr Williams was a considerable and enduring influence on a whole generation of young people, as well as being a constant source of laughter and enjoyment. We would all go for long hikes in the country, more than once missing the last bus or train home, and occasionally would be taken for a week to a cottage at the head of Thirlmere in the Lake District for more sustained fell-walking.

One Saturday I was unusually invited for a country walk with Geoffrey on my own. He and Dennis Eastwood had clearly been discussing me, for Mr Eastwood had asked only a few days earlier the same question Geoffrey was to put to me. Had I ever thought of ordination?

My first reaction was incredulity. 'Could you see me drinking tea with old ladies?' And anyway, had I not decided to make the RAF my career? And could I not serve God in that vocation just as much as in the priesthood? But the seed had been sown, and nagged away – irritatingly – in the background, quite refusing to go away. And when God made it clear that for a minor medical reason which never gave me a moment's trouble I could not be a pilot in the Air Force, it was a clear sign which I accepted immediately: it was not what *I* wanted to do which mattered, but what God purposed for me.

RAF pilots get killed and so my mother was not displeased when I was rejected, though deeply worried about the medical cause, for in those days tuberculosis was a major killer. My father assumed that I could not have made the decision to seek ordination without undue influence from Geoffrey Williams, and hoped it was 'another craze' which would eventually go away.

I had completed two years in the sixth form with what would now be considered as one B and one C at A level. But in those far-off days we sat for Higher School Certificate and must achieve three passes at the same examination – which I had not done. Geography had let me down, even though I had thought it the best paper I had ever written, and I have never understood or believed in my failure. So after discharge from the RAF I returned to school to re-sit the three papers – English Literature, Geography and French.

It was also decided (or rather my mother decided) that we should move house, to a part of Bury higher up and therefore with clearer air than Parkhills Road. My father was a creature of habit and his resistance created the only barrier I ever knew to exist between my parents. For whether it was because the safety valve of argument which many couples need was amply fulfilled through Grandma, or whether it was simply that they were just not the sort of married couple who engaged in verbal violence, I do not know. Whatever the reason I cannot recall them having a single row.

But we did move, about the end of 1949, to 1 West Drive, Seedfield in north Bury – a more prestigious address which marked a growing prosperity in my father's business. Grandma, of course, came to live with us, but it was our own house, and it gave my mother great happiness in her last years. But at first my father was desperately homesick for the old house, and was seen returning to it, just to open the front gate and walk up to the door.

In the meanwhile, I began to apply for a university place and was awarded one at University College, Durham, on condition that I passed my Higher School Certificate. This time, in July 1950, my failure was entirely my own fault. I had just finished my French examination when I realised I should have written it on two separate sheets for different examiners to mark. I almost reached the pass mark on the first paper alone, so with the two I ought to have had a creditable result. Instead I failed, and it seemed an insurmountable crisis.

'Well, that's that,' my father said with a smug satisfaction which I found hurtful. I could join him in the family business and all the nonsense of university and ordination would have to be put aside. 'That certainly isn't that,' I replied, and we had a violent shouting argument. He was my father and why didn't I ever come to him for advice? I should forget all these fancy ideas and come down to earth. Of course I couldn't go to university now that I had failed yet again. What did he know about it and I'd show him what I could do. And so on.

Time, of course, was short: the results had been declared in mid-August and university terms started in October, so that many of those responsible for admissions were on vacation. I was advised to write again to Durham, but also to apply to King's College, London and St David's College, Lampeter, with as full a *curriculum vitae* as I could muster.

I heard first of all from Lampeter, from the principal, Dr Archdall, offering me a place for that October. By then it was September, and so I accepted it. A couple of weeks later I heard from Durham that they could also offer me a place, and later still received a characteristically warm and welcoming letter from Dean Eric Abbott of King's, London. Against headmasterly and clerical advice, I decided to hold to the Lampeter offer, since I had accepted when other doors seemed closed. It was a degree course particularly suited to an ordinand, and I have never regretted my decision.

Chapter five

To Be a Pale Young Curate

I started as a freshman at Lampeter in October 1950. Now part of the University of Wales, St David's College was founded as a place of higher education for poor Welsh boys unable to afford places at 'either of the other two universities', and had been granted the right to award degrees by Queen Victoria.

In 1950, the majority of students were ordinands and it was said that fifty per cent of Welsh clergy wives were daughters of the town – hard to believe, given the restrictions on fraternisation with the opposite sex! We were forbidden on pain of expulsion even to allow female relatives into our rooms. College gates were locked at 8 p.m. in winter and 9.30 p.m. in summer, after which we were allowed out only to visit another student in lodgings, or, once a week, to go to the cinema show at the village hall. We were forbidden to attend the parish church but required to be 'marked into chapel' for three Mattins and three Evensongs each week, in addition to Sung Mattins every Sunday.

The vice-principal was the Professor of Welsh, the Reverend W.H. Harris, a vigorous gallophile known to all as 'Pa Bill'. I fell foul of him quite inadvertently. For some quaint reason, he introduced a rule that no one should kneel for prayer before leaving the college chapel. One day, without thinking, I knelt as soon as those who had conducted the service had processed out. Pa Bill had tiny eyes with which he could read only by holding the book an inch from his face. But he saw more than we imagined and was waiting for me as soon as I came out of chapel. I was to go immediately to his study.

He made me wait a while and then called me in. Did I not know the rules? Yes, but ... But nothing! Rules were meant to be obeyed. I had always been taught to say a prayer after worship and it was an automatic reaction. Nonsense, it was deliberate disobedience. Was I not happy at Lampeter? Then I must obey the rules. And if it happened again, I would find myself before the College Board, faced with possible expulsion. As he harangued me, it struck me that, in his cassock and Canterbury cap, he greatly resembled Grandma.

I played hockey in winter and tennis in summer, and away fixtures provided a temporary release from the stifling restrictions of the college. Since we were forbidden to enter any licensed bar within five miles of Lampeter (except, for some perverse reason, the railway refreshment room – the line from Aberystwyth to Carmarthen was still open), there was never any problem about filling team coaches with supporters.

Meanwhile, on a snowy New Year's Day in 1951, I went to a CACTM selection conference at Farnham Castle, then the home of the Bishop of Guildford. It was a strange experience, not unlike the ACCM Conference described by A.N. Wilson in his novel, *Unguarded Hours*. The chairman was a bishop, who asked me if I liked cricket. Honesty was, I thought, the best policy. No, I found it totally boring. Fortunately he said he did too, and from then we got on famously. The layman, a major-general, seemed troubled that I hadn't been to a public school, but thought it wouldn't matter too much so long as I didn't read theology. The academic also felt that ordinands should not read theology and was a little concerned that I proposed to major in philosophy. Somehow I was accepted, and years later the secretary, Philip Wheeldon, told me I had left them no choice. What he could have meant I have no idea.

It was at Lampeter that I first encountered the foolishness of class distinction – and learned that it mattered only to those who aspired to be 'better' than they were. It was really confined to those who had attended minor rather than major public schools, and one could only be sorry for them. More difficult were the barriers created by regional accents. Having now lived for most of my life away from Lancashire, my Lancashire accent has been neutered by other local influences – though I find that professional actors or broadcasters I meet do still detect it, if sometimes they cannot readily identify its origin. In 1950, it was strong and undiminished, not popular for lesson reading in chapel and quite unacceptable for the college dramatic society, though I was allowed to help back-stage.

It was at Lampeter too that I first encountered churchmanship. There were, I discovered, signs and symbols that identified one's ecclesiastical preferences. Why did some students kneel at the *Incarnatus* in the Creed? Why did others find problems in obeying the college rule that they must turn eastwards when reciting the Creed? Why did some bow to the altar and others ostentatiously ignore it?

For no other reason than that my life seemed to need it, I soon fell into the practice of attending three or four mornings a week for Holy Communion, a voluntary service which preceded the partly compulsory Mattins. I was surprised when I found that this labelled me as 'High Church', and intensely annoyed when I discovered that evangelicals in a prayer group were consequently praying for my conversion. The 'Low Church' aversion to symbols seemed excessive and unhelpful and by my third year I had discovered – rather to my surprise – that I was a catholic.

I joined the Anglo-catholic Society of St David and if I shut my eyes to the lacy camp flummery of its more extreme members, I found that the dignity of catholic worship exactly fitted my spiritual needs. And catholics anyway had the best sense of humour, an essential virtue in any Christian.

I also, with some reluctance, made my first confession – to a Bury priest during an Easter vacation. A fellow-student, Raymond Avent – now a priest and noted retreat-conductor – did so too, and remarked with wonder at God's absolution: 'Will it always feel so good?' No, I can say after nearly forty years of receiving the sacrament of penance. But only because that wonder has been transformed in the knowledge that God's love bears every hurt our sins can impose and still accepts us as we are and not as he would wish us to be.

The discovery of catholicism naturally influenced my choice of theological college, and in those days the choice was wider. Salisbury and Wells both had a moderate catholic tradition – surprising to those who know the joint Salisbury-Wells College of today with its reputation as one of the most extreme liberal establishments. The pre-1960 Cuddesdon too, under its principal Edward Knapp-Fisher, was catholic, though – rightly or not – non-Oxbridge, non-public-school ordinands were advised to avoid it. Westcott House in Cambridge was glibly (and perhaps inaccurately?) dismissed as a 'country club for ecclesiastically-minded young gentlemen'. St Stephen's House, Oxford, was 'too high' and Mirfield full of monastic restrictions.

I decided to aim for Chichester: it was catholic without too many frills; the principal, Dr John Moorman, a historian of repute; it was the oldest theological college, founded in 1839 by some of the fathers of the Oxford Movement; and after the delightful countryside around Lampeter it would be good to sample the beauties of Sussex. Dr Moorman interviewed me in Rylands Library in Manchester and offered me a place for August 1953 which I quickly accepted. It was the beginning of two happy years.

With the post-war era only a few years old, students were on average more mature and certainly more varied in their backgrounds and experience. At Lampeter we still suffered from rationing and queued at the buttery every week for our two-ounce butter ration and a tiny bag of sugar, but by 1953 food supplies were almost normal. At both Lampeter and Chichester many students were veterans of the war, older men who had between them fought in every theatre of action and in each of the services. It was good for those of us who came straight from school or National Service, and their maturity tempered our immaturity.

Fr Edward Maycock was vice-principal and Jim Hannon the chaplain, and as well as the full-time staff, others came in on a part-time basis. Of these the most noteworthy was undoubtedly Canon W.K. Lowther-Clarke, a biblical scholar of great renown who in 1952 had produced his own complete Concise Bible Commentary. Dr Lowther-Clarke was, moreover, a man of great piety and was an important example of the central purpose of our training at Chichester – that a priest is to be a man of prayer.

The college programme was centred on prayer: daily Mass, Mattins and meditation before breakfast; a midday office; Evensong before supper and then at 9 p.m. the late evening office of Compline, followed by silence until after breakfast. Even though my understanding of the nature of prayer has developed over the years, I know that my priesthood would have little reality without the foundation given to me by Chichester.

Otherwise the rules were less restrictive than at Lampeter and had a sound logic behind them. We could buy alcohol at supper but were not allowed to visit public houses, on the grounds that, if we did, it would quickly be said that 'those theological students are never out of pubs'. I believe this was right, and on the same basis have never visited pubs in my own parishes, save on the rarest of special occasions.

If relations with the opposite sex were to be circumspect, at least they were not forbidden, and the unmarried among us were frequent visitors at Bishop Otter College, then a women's teacher training college. So far as I know, wedding bells never rang, but it was not for want of trying. In any event, I think it gave comfort to Dr Moorman, who had a fear of any of his young men getting involved in homosexual activities. Of that he had no cause for concern amongst my contemporaries. But he did give wise words of warning in pastoral addresses about the dangers of too close relationships in parochial work with members of either sex, for the avoidance of the tragedies which do occur all too often in the priesthood. He would be deeply – and rightly – shocked at the licence permitted in clerical discipline in these 'liberated' days.

His favourite exhortation to those in his charge was even more telling: 'Never be a *busy* priest.' Even those most adept in not being 'busy' will be greeted by the kind parishioner, 'I know you're very busy, but ...' Though that cannot be avoided, Moorman was right: the priest who can never see a needy parishioner until a week on Friday, whose diary is so full that there is no space for people, whose wife and family can only be slotted in for a reluctant ten minutes every other day, is failing in his ministry. Chichester taught me that we are people – often indeed the only people – with a work-load that can give time for others. When I find the pages of my diary filling up well into the future, I hear the quiet, kindly voice of John Moorman: 'George, don't be a busy priest.'

My final year at Chichester was marred by two operations and seven weeks in hospital, and dominated of course by my mother's terminal illness. She died on Sunday, 24th April 1955, and I returned for my final term immediately after the funeral. I was also forced to consider where I should serve my title.

Manchester was my home diocese but was, I felt, too small for me to get far enough away from my home doorstep, and I had been accepted for ordination by the Blackburn diocese. Bishop Baddeley interviewed me during the Easter vacation, just before my mother's death. And I had a problem: I had discovered that I had been 'dedicated' at Christian Church Baptists but of course not baptised. But I had been confirmed, and for several years had been receiving Holy Communion. The Bishop said that I must go for baptism to the priest who prepared me for confirmation and then, as I was to be ordained, he would then confirm me conditionally in his chapel 'just to be on the safe side'. My father naturally thought the confusion was my fault: 'You never get owt the right way round!' Certainly I must be the only unbaptised person to have been accepted by ACCM. Or perhaps not these days.

The Bishop asked me to look at three parishes: St Peter's Fleetwood, Clitheroe, and St Peter's Chorley. My spiritual director at that time was Fr Leslie Pickett, vicar of Holy Trinity Bury (which I had come to regard as my home parish). He was a fine priest and I own much to him; but under his firm catholic armour was a curious puritanical streak. For he was of the firm conviction, particularly so far as the priestly life was concerned, that if it was enjoyable it was somehow contrary to the will of God. When I asked how I could be sure which parish God wanted me to serve in, he was quite clear: 'Look for the least attractive – that will be God's will for you.' It was disastrous advice.

I arranged to go first to Fleetwood. There was a sensible catholic tradition, very like Chichester; plenty of scope, with the parish covering the whole town; and a vicar whom I knew I could respect, even though he fell asleep during the interview. He had others to see and would let me know: and I hoped he would make me the offer.

Then I went to Chorley. I did not like the church or the churchmanship (vaguely but – I suspected – only outwardly catholic); I did not like the vicar; I did not like the accommodation; I did not relish the fact that the former curate was now the Bishop's chaplain; and I did not like Chorley. If Fr Pickett had given me a check-list, St Peter's Chorley would have entirely fitted. It must surely be God's will for me, for nowhere could be less attractive. I accepted, and if I was aware of the unease of the staff at Chichester, it would not have made me change my mind. I felt a glow of pride that I had been holy enough to make so great and noble a sacrifice for God.

I was made deacon in Blackburn Cathedral on 5th June 1955. My father was there, Joe Shaw, now retired from Arsenal and living in Ripon, and many other friends. I felt my mother was not far away and was with me in prayer.

The vicar of St Peter's was the Reverend Harry Simpson, and we met as vicar and curate for the first time on the Monday morning for the weekly staff meeting. I was given a visiting list which looked likely to keep me busy for the remainder of the year – and two funerals. The first of these was that same day, when I had to supervise the committal of a Methodist corpse into the churchyard. I assumed it was just a matter of accompanying the minister to the grave and staying while he said the words of committal. It was my first blunder. It might be a Methodist body and a Methodist minister but it was an Anglican churchyard. *I* was to say the words of committal from the Prayer Book and the Methodist must not be allowed to utter a word of prayer of any kind. Had I been ordained for this kind of pettiness, I wondered. But I kept my peace, and with some embarrassment, did as I was told.

I was only able to visit for the second funeral after dark. It was a tiny cottage, lit only by oil-lamps, and the ancient widow led me upstairs to 'see 'im'. Funeral customs vary from place to place but in a Lancashire working-class parish in 1955 everyone had to view the body. The face was always covered with a cream silk handkerchief and one had to lift it gently away and make appropriate comments, followed, in the case of a minister, by a prayer.

Bereavement rituals are not to be despised, for they are a necessary part of recovery. But I could not help thinking with a smile of how as a child I had been taken to view Uncle Will, and wondering how otherwise I should have coped with this eerie room with the cadaver lit only by a flickering taper.

On my first Sunday, I found that what had been described by the Bishop's chaplain (my predecessor) as a 'grand and growing Parish Communion' was something of a romp. There was little sense of mystery or catholic worship, innumerable hymns, and a five-minute chat from the vicar; but a crowded church too, and lots of young people (who were to be one of my concerns) and a sense of belonging.

In the evening I preached my first sermon at Evensong and fondly imagined that I had another month before the next one (the Bishop's rule for deacons was one sermon a month for the first six months, then one every two weeks). I could not have been more mistaken: at Monday's staff meeting, I was told I would be preaching on alternate Sundays at the Parish communion and on the other weeks at Evensong.

The folk were kindly enough and some became great friends. One of the first whom I met was Jean Royle with her little daughter Anne (one day to marry a priest's son) and son Kevin (now himself a priest in Blackburn). Jean's husband, Brian, was on the PCC. We still correspond at Christmas.

There were pitfalls to be avoided by the keen young curate. One organisation strong in the parish was the Sons of Temperance, a friendly society unfriendly towards the demon drink, and the Sunday School Superintendent, Horace Hough, was its Grand Scribe. An elderly member, Miss Major, lived alone in a detached part of the parish and one cold day I visited her. Would I like some of her home-made wine rather than a cup of tea? I would but – 'Wine, and you a Daughter of Temperance?' 'Oh, Mr Austin, it's not real wine – just something I've made from potatoes.' She gave me a glass. It was tasteless and seemed innocuous, so I had a second. And a third. Eventually I left for home. As I walked into the cold evening air, I stumbled and my head swam. A hangover from potato wine is not to be recommended. Never again did I taste a temperance brew.

By September I knew I had made a terrible mistake. How could I endure two more years of Chorley? I think the vicar and I both tried to make the best of it, at any rate during the first twelve months.

Parochial church council meetings were monthly crosses to bear, but I learned that curates were to be seen and not heard and could relax. I took the same relaxed attitude to my first Annual Church Meeting: it was a major blunder. It was the custom, so I learned, for votes of thanks to be given to all and sundry, and I listened with interest, knowing I did not have a role in the exercise. Then the vicar called for a vote of thanks for the treasurer. No one spoke. I let my eyes wander round with interest, wondering who was asleep. The vicar said, rather nastily, 'Well, if Mr Austin won't do it, I suppose I must. But I would have thought he would show less ingratitude to the man who pays him his monthly cheque!'

The following May, during the ordination retreat, each of the candidates for the priesthood had a half-hour interview with the Bishop. 'I want you to tell me exactly how it has been – remember I'm your Father-in-God. You can speak quite freely and in absolute confidence.' So I did. By the following Thursday I had heard from two priests at opposite ends of the diocese that the Bishop was very angry with me, that there was nothing wrong with the parish and I should be glad to be there, and that I was making a mountain out of a molehill. It was my first experience of the truism that a weak bishop will always prefer the voice that tells him what he wants to hear – and my Bishop had at his side my predecessor who had nothing but good to say of St Peter's Chorley.

The moment I found I could not trust the Bishop, I decided that I would leave the parish and the diocese at the earliest opportunity. But after ordination to the priesthood on Sunday, 27th May 1956, there was still a long, long year to serve before that happy day.

Now that I was in priest's orders I was more use to the vicar. He was chaplain to Eaves Lane Hospital and now, as well as visiting each week, I was allowed to go at 5.30 every Tuesday morning for the weekly Communion service on the wards. I ran the Youth Club on a Sunday evening and did weddings and baptisms and confirmation classes and taught in the church schools and prepared the Sunday school teachers and sat through meetings of the Mothers' Union and Men's Society and Young Wives (none of whom could meet validly without the full-time presence of one of us) and chaplained the choir and visited thirty homes a week and went to bed exhausted every night.

To give him his due, the vicar worked just as hard, rarely taking a day off. The Bishop had ruled that curates were required to have a day off each week and three Sundays a year for holidays, so much as the vicar disapproved he could do little about it.

We did have a minor altercation after my priest's ordination when he 'suggested' that this Sunday should count as one of my three holiday Sundays. I simply asked that he write to the Bishop for a ruling, and no more was heard of that!

Some time during the year, as I learned from my old landlady after I had left the parish, the vicar reported me to the Bishop. 'He's terrible,' the verger had told her. 'You know the vicar's had to write to the Bishop about him.' I never knew why and never bothered to find out, I had by then, anyway, further upset the Bishop. We had gone to a diocesan overseas mission service in Blackpool at which the Bishop of Blackburn was to preach. The church was crowded and we were in the middle of the nave and in the middle of a pew.

The Bishop was in his element when he preached on overseas missions and he even more easily brought the subject round to his beloved Melanesian Mission. As he continued – at some length – I began to feel sick from the sea-front fish and chips I had had for lunch, and hoped I could hold out until the end of the service. It was not to be: my stomach retched and my mouth began to fill with saliva and I knew I must get outside as quickly as possible.

Unfortunately, the Bishop had reached the point in his sermon when he made his challenge: 'Perhaps there is a young priest in this congregation here today who will come forward and offer himself for service in the Pacific Islands.' I stood up and clambered hastily over the knees of the people between me and the aisle. All eyes were on me. The Bishop stopped in mid-sentence and watched – with eagerness turning to surprise and then to anger – as I reached the end of the pew and rushed up the aisle and out of the church with my hand clutched over my lips. After that, he could never possibly forgive me.

When 1957 came, I began more seriously to look for a second curacy. Fr Pickett suggested I might go to see an old friend of his, Fr Ronald Arthur, who was vicar of St Clement's Notting Dale in the diocese of London – what in today's jargon would be described as an inner-city parish with a multi-racial, multi-cultural situation. I went to see him during my Easter break and found a jolly bachelor priest with whom I knew I could work very happily.

My two-year title finished on Trinity Sunday 1957 and I left Chorley on the Monday morning at nine o'clock, laden with a surprising number of gifts and much kindness and goodwill from the people of St Peter's. When I returned to preach at Evensong thirty years to the day after my first sermon, I found old friends there – and not a few middle-aged men and women who told me they were in the Youth Club all those years ago. The surprising thing was that I recognised and remembered them. And it was encouraging to find that many of the names of PCC members were familiar as Youth Club members. Perhaps I didn't put too many off the Christian life after all.

There could not have been a greater contrast to St Peter's than the parish of St Clement's Notting Dale. Lying just north of Shepherd's Bush, Notting Dale was in the early nineteenth century on the edge of built-up London. Those who came to the great city expecting to find the streets paved with gold often found a roof in Notting Dale, and some older inhabitants still had a trace of a country burr in their speech. Gypsies, too, had settled there, first in caravans and then in the tiny houses, and occasionally I would visit one of them, Cinderella Smith, who was then over a hundred years old. Unlike other parts of North Kensington, Notting Dale had never seen better days and in the early years of this century had been described as the 'Avernus of Kensington'.

Much of the housing has now been replaced by modern terracing and tower blocks, but in 1957 it was a place of mean streets, violence and poverty – and of people with hearts of gold. I loved it, and soon settled into the parish routine – very different from Chorley. Now crowds did not flock to church, and house-to-house visiting became a grinding and unrewarding chore. But of ministry there was much, and now mainly to those outside the family of the church.

Funeral traditions vary widely, and here at my first interment I was amazed to find the cortège making a stop at a public house. We drew to a halt and the funeral director climbed out of the hearse to stand, head bared and bowed. Across the road outside the pub was the landlord with his wife, also bare-headed and downcast in respect. I asked the driver what was going on. He explained that this was the deceased's pub and it was the custom to make a pause in such circumstances.

The vicarage had been designed as a clergy house so that the curates could live on the premises. I had a large sitting-room with a partitioned bedroom *en suite* and I ate each day with the vicar. We had a housekeeper – or rather a succession of housekeepers, good, bad and indifferent, until a parishioner, Mrs Harris, red-faced and full of laughter, took over and we never looked back.

I quickly settled into a routine of worship not unlike that at college – Mattins, daily Mass and Evensong – and rarely did we meet for any of the daily offices without the presence of lay folk from the congregation. On Sunday the main service was a Sung Mass – incense and much catholic ritual, but still 'Prayer Book' (with additions) and only moderately high by London standards. It was poorly attended, with a small but intensely faithful congregation of all ages, and had the 1968 pastoral Measure been in operation then one would have judged it ripe for redundancy.

I returned some twenty-five years later for a ninetieth birthday party of one of the ladies and found a thriving, busy congregation. Good work certainly there had been by recent clergy serving there: but that modern congregation owed much to those few faithful folk who brought the parish to God and God to the parish in the lean days of the 1950s. Notting Dale taught me that there is more to the Church than large numbers, and confirmed me in the view that God expects of his chosen not that they be successful but that they are faithful.

I was still desperately poor, even though the curate's scale in the London diocese was much more realistic than that in Blackburn. The purchasing power of £450 per annum in 1957 would be a little over £4,000 in 1990 terms. Wages were generally lower than today, but it is some comparison that a mentally retarded lad of twenty who worked as a cleaner at the local police station earned more than I did. We were exploited by the Church of God.

Because we were a poor parish, we often received gifts of clothes which had belonged to the departed of the more affluent areas of Kensington. An elderly parishioner used to organise their distribution and one day she came to me, rather hesitantly. She hoped I did not mind her saying so, but she had noticed my shoes were in a poor state and my dressing gown falling to pieces (how *did* she know that?). There was a good pair of shoes and a dressing gown in the latest batch of clothes and it would please her if I would take them. It cost me no pride to accept her kindness.

I now listen with a wry smile when well-heeled bishops and socially responsible clergy lecture the General Synod about poverty. It is true that I never wanted for food and that my experience only brought me to the distant fringe of what passes for poverty in the affluent West. But it was real, and it was unpleasant, and it taught me that poverty does not ennoble.

At the same time I could not believe that God cared more for me because I was poor than he cared for the rich who lived among the bright lights and expensive properties of Holland Park a quarter of a mile away. I could not worship and serve a God who had a bias towards the poor or the rich or the black or the white, and the seed of that understanding was sown in me in the poverty I shared with the folk of St Clement's parish in the late 1950s.

One event was to have a profound effect on my future life as a priest. Those seeking London's gold pavements still settled in North Kensington, but by now it was the immigrant people from the West Indies. The fashionable term for ethnic groups changes, so that yesterday's requirement becomes today's insult. 'Afro-Caribbean' may well be replaced, as in its turn it made 'black' –

the OK word of the Seventies – as socially unacceptable as 'negro'. In the late 1950s 'black' had once before been superseded by 'coloured'. However incredible to modern ears, it was racist to use any other description than 'coloured', and 'coloured' immigration was the hottest political potato.

In Notting Dale it was simply a fact of life – at least until a hot September Saturday in 1958. I had said the eight o'clock Mass on the Sunday morning and after breakfast took a telephone call from a journalist. Was I going to preach on race relations? Hadn't I heard the riots? Certainly I was conscious that there had been a good deal of noise around midnight. But that was nothing unusual in Notting Dale. Usually on Saturday night (though not on that one) we were serenaded by Jimmy Mac's father, a genial Scotsman who considered it part of a drunken night out to call at the clergy house and entertain us with a song. At midnight. And there were often fights, and more than once I had gone out to separate the combatants.

But riots? Yet on that Saturday night, gangs of youths had sought out and beaten people walking alone or in pairs for no better reason than that their skin was black. And having started, the riots continued, night after night, until the fire was dampened by several evenings of torrential rain. By modern standards they were fairly mild, and confined to a small area centred on Notting Dale. At their height, I saw a coloured man in Lancaster Road beaten to the ground by a youth wielding a dustbin lid, while only a hundred yards around the corner in Ladbroke Grove, West Indians safely waited at bus stops.

The police were out in force, unprotected by – and without the need for – riot shields and the essential modern paraphernalia of today's lethal conflicts. I could stand on a doorstep between a West Indian family and the mob with little danger to myself, for the presence of a priest in a cassock was enough to deter the violence.

But it was an ugly upsurge and even the congregation at St Clement's was divided on the issue of race relations. The Church centrally was ambivalent and some of the local clergy positively hostile. Fortunately the Bishop of Kensington, Cyril Eastaugh (who later became Bishop of Peterborough), lived in nearby Notting Hill and could not have been more supportive. But secular groups and individuals moved in with a vengeance. For some it provided an ideal scenario to experiment with their pet social theory, and it was my first encounter with the truth that for some of the Concerned Classes, the cause is more important than individuals. But others came genuinely to help and none more unstintingly than musicians and entertainers.

The guiding spirit among these was the late Alexis Korner who lived nearby, and who with broadcaster and then saxophonist, Benny Green, brought black and white musicians to play gigs in scruffy church halls. It was a small gesture and its effectiveness cannot be judged. But they did treat the community as people rather than as a faceless social problem. And a few violent young folk talked with musicians they respected who happened to have a skin of another colour.

Fr Trevor Huddleston was then Prior of the Community of the Resurrection house in Holland Park and an invaluable resource for bringing groups together with mutually-useful expertise. I had become involved in two local youth clubs, of which one, run by Rugby School on highly paternalistic lines, was well-equipped and catered for a large youth membership, some of whom had impressive police records. Fr Huddleston deeply impressed the youth club lads with his readiness to take on the racist political venom they had been imbibing and which had encouraged them on to the streets. He arranged two further visits and it was unfortunate that he was forced to withdraw, first because of an invitation to speak to the senior boys at Eton and then because of a television appearance. Unreasonably, when I told the youth club I would try to arrange another date, they refused to welcome him again and an opportunity was lost just as they were beginning to hear a different message.

The area was also invaded by the political right, adding explosive to an already volatile situation. The British National Party opened a bookshop in nearby Princedale Road, while in 1959 Sir Oswald Mosley appeared as a parliamentary candidate. Through Trevor Huddleston I had come to know his son, the writer Nicholas Mosley, now Lord Ravensdale. His political outlook was anything but that of Sir Oswald, and during the election campaign it was fascinating to stand with Nick in a darkened shop doorway observing his father's street-corner meetings, with a running commentary from Nick.

The Union Movement's second-in-command, Jeffrey Hamm, would first rouse the crowd and nothing would be seen of Mosley himself. After ten or fifteen minutes of this, Nick whispered to me, 'Now watch the end of one of the streets. My father will suddenly appear, and Hamm will stop in mid-sentence.' And so it was – brilliantly stage-managed. Mosley would climb on to the platform amid cheers and for another ten or twenty minutes the oratory would flow, every sentence a drop of poison. Fortunately North Kensington was a safe Labour seat and Mosley was defeated.

In 1958 a new priest came on to the scene – I think through the encouragement of the Bishop – as curate at St Michael's Ladbroke Grove. Randolph George was West Indian born and, with his gentle dignity and humour, quietly brought a new dimension into local church life. And we were able occasionally to share a day off. Randolph recently reminded me – on a visit to England from Guyana, where he is now Bishop – that I used to badger him into joining me at the theatre. We are now both married and it is hard for either of us to recall that a curate in inner-city London, neither married nor gay, can have a lonely life. The post which was to follow, as assistant chaplain in the University of London, was anything but lonely. But before that was to happen, two major influences were to impinge on my Christian and priestly life.

Chapter six

Swedes and Turn-ups

God may use the weak things of this world to confound the
wisdom of the mighty: but he also uses the most unlikely and
minor of incidents to transform the paths we take in our lives.
Notting Dale provided me with three: one practical, one theological and one for controversy.

One afternoon in early 1959, I delayed starting a round of
visits in order to hear the end of a concert on the radio. When it
was over, I was just about to open the front door when the door-
bell rang. To my astonishment, standing there was the eccentric
figure of the redoubtable Rosamund Essex, then editor of the
Church Times.

I explained that the vicar was already out on his rounds, but
she had in fact turned up to see me, to talk about the riots, their
background, the church's involvement, and so on, for an article
she proposed to write. We went to my study and talked for
nearly an hour. Then she studied me pensively for a long minute.
Would I write the article? I wouldn't know how. Yes, I could:
she had seen examples of my writing (where? I wondered) and
knew I could do it.

Of course I did write the article, and after that others, though
never then (or for that matter since) did I write anything I did not
believe would be rejected. I tell myself that such a lack of confidence is necessary if the best is to be achieved, though I have little
confidence in my own advice.

As a result of the *Church Times* articles, I began to be asked to
speak at meetings and rallies on the race issue in general and on the
particular situation in Notting Hill, and I came to see the

difference of presentation between simply recounting a dry fact of doctrine in a sermon and speaking from the heart on an issue of moment. Yet I believed no less in the truths of the gospel than in the fact that racism was an evil. And there were plenty of particular stories and instances both from Scripture and from daily life to bring colour and interest to sermons. Did I not believe enough? Did the gospel of salvation in fact not excite me?

Fortunately, so far as presentation was concerned, the riots opened one door which over the years was to be a constant source of experience, at least in the art of preaching. A year after the riots, I was contacted by Michael Redington, the religious affairs producer for Associated Television, to take part in a live discussion on the issue. It was in the days before video recordings and I suspect that ours was a stilted performance to modern standards. I know I felt I had been woolly and indecisive in responding to the chairman, Tom Driberg's, questions. Nevertheless, Michael Redington phoned the next day to ask if I would join the Saturday evening Epilogue panel and I became a regular contributor for the next three or four years – in fact until a new producer came on the scene and sacked the entire panel.

It was hardly surprising that he should remove us, for we were in all honesty rather amateurish. The Epilogue was always live, in so far as anyone is sufficiently alive to speak about religion at midnight. We used the announcer's tiny studio, and after his farewell to listeners, he would announce that in a moment would follow the Epilogue. As thousands of hands stretched out to switch off thousands of TV sets, the camera was manhandled 180 degrees and were launched into our two-minute slot. It was a brainwave of Shaw Taylor, then one of the announcers, which gained us an audience. One Saturday evening when I was on duty he suggested that I sit beside him rather than opposite. At the end of the evening's programmes, he would then turn to me and say, 'Finally, here with me in the studio is ...' And thousands of hands hesitated. Television's hypnotic spell was unbroken, and at least there was someone there to listen.

It was some years later that I began to contribute to BBC Radio Four's *Prayer for the Day*. Michael Mayne had been a member of the Epilogue panel and was by then Head of Religious Broadcasting for BBC Radio, and living in the diocese of St Albans where I then was serving. He rang one day to ask if I would like to write a few scripts for consideration and send them to the *Prayer for the Day* producer, Fr Pat MacEnroe. With some effort, I eventually did so and Fr Pat wrote back kindly – but not at all to my surprise – to say they were no good. Would I try again? I did so. And again. It was useless, I told Fr Pat, I didn't have the knack. He thought I could do it, and would I try just once more? This time it worked, and I contributed for several years until the producer changed.

There is a gentle BBC *Yes, Minister* technique which bears no comparison with the harsher dismissal of fading contributors employed by Associated Television. 'Of course you haven't been dropped, you're too valuable, and we'll soon be contacting you again, just be patient.' It is right that the same voices should not be heard for too long, and one's pride is preserved at the same time.

In 1980, Pauline Webb was appointed as head of the Religious Department of the BBC World Service, and to my surprise – and to the anger of some of the staff of the British Council of Churches who disapproved of my views – asked me to contribute to *Reflections*, a daily slot similar to Radio Four's *Thought for the Day* but recorded the previous day. This was a more demanding broadcast: not only was it written under last-minute pressure and with a need to combine current affairs with theological comment, it was for the very different – and a potential thirty million – audience of the World Service. Many did not have English as their first language, so there was a need for a detailed examination to excise the obscure phrase or insular reference, with a delicate sensitivity to the effect of incautious comments. Moreover, I began to realise that the discipline of broadcasting from a prepared text was feeding into my technique as a preacher.

Before a recording Pauline or her assistant, Ron Farrow, would look carefully at my script. This was not an exercise in censorship: indeed I cannot recall a single occasion when Pauline agreed with what I had said. Rather it was to improve technique and presentation: 'This phrase says a second time what you've already said once; that sentence distracts from the main point; put the clauses of that phrase the other way round and it will make more impact; re-write the opening if you want to keep the audience's attention.'

Later I was asked to join the *Thought for the Day* panel, broadcasting always live on the BBC morning flagship news and current affairs programme, Radio Four's *Today*. Part of the understanding for contributors is that if a new story breaks which will dominate the next morning's programme, you will be telephoned by the producer and – whatever the time – you will have to rewrite the script. Only once has this happened to me: when the IRA bombed the Carlton Club.

The adrenalin must flow in the veins of *Thought for the Day* contributors and I am always glad that Brian Redhead's friendly (and sometimes outrageous!) comments beforehand aid the process. And as with the World Service, there is the help and advice of the producers of *Thought*. I am old enough now for them to appear ridiculously young, though I suppose most are in their mid- to late-twenties. I wish that at theological college, staff could have spent the time and given the highly professional help in sermon preparation that I have received from the producers at the BBC.

It is nevertheless somewhat alarming that a very controversial contribution (usually the script one feels is least so!) will produce an avalanche of correspondence. Ten per cent will be in support; 20 per cent written in green ink underlined in red and incomprehensible; and much of the remainder attacking the contributor for saying the exact opposite of what was actually said. The nastiest letters come from fellow-Christians, are written on re-cycled paper, and can usually be identified by the stick-on label on the envelope, embellished by the picture of a tree in full leaf.

But there is a pastoral side: people do write who would not speak face-to-face with a dog-collared vicar, and in preparing a script or in answering correspondence, one must be aware of the listener or writer. Once, having spoken about violence against children, I had been home from the studio only a short time when the phone rang. It was a man who introduced himself as a member of the Jewish community, whose small child had been murdered the previous week. My heart stopped: I hoped I hadn't added to his grief. Not at all, he wanted to thank me for what I had said. And we were able to talk for some twenty minutes, he to a voice to which he could not put a face, from a religious community to which he did not belong – and this, I think, was a help in his bereavement. For me, it was a reminder that we speak to an audience we cannot see but of whose needs and pains and griefs and expectations we must be aware.

But the discipline of producing a script timed to the second, whether the four minutes fifteen seconds of the World Service or the two minutes fifty-five for Radio Four, has given me an added bonus. For it has – by some curious mental quirk – given me the knack of preaching without notes. This is not to be recommended for the newcomer to preaching, for its pitfalls are waffle, repetition and the temptation not to prepare. Yet, dangers apart, to have come to be able to do it has, I know, transformed my sermons.

The clergy are no less professionally performers than actors and broadcasters, and much that we do in church worship would benefit if we recognised that it was the activity of a professional wordsmith. To replace the Authorised Version of the Bible with a modern translation and the Prayer Book with the Alternative Service Book is of little advantage if we read it without preparation, without care and sometimes apparently without understanding.

Worse still, it is not uncommon for the clergy to despise such professionalism, as if there could be something creditable in declaiming the word and worship of God in a third-rate manner. With some it expands into a hostility towards the media as a whole. Once, when walking with a Channel 4 News producer to an outside location for filming a contribution to an extended item on the church, I asked her if she had had difficulty in setting up the interviews. 'I have never met such difficulty and antagonism, even from the Health Service (*sic*!),' she replied.

If the clergy are hostile to broadcasters, their attitude is positively benign by comparison with the almost pathological contempt in which they hold journalists. In the coffee room at the General Synod, I was once astonished by the Jekyll-and-Hyde-transformation which overcame a well-known bishop when he realised that the young woman with whom he was talking – all smiles and pleasantry – was from a (quality) Sunday newspaper. That a Christian bishop could treat a fellow human being with such open contempt was not only highly embarrassing but also a matter for deep concern. What impression did she (a non-Christian as it happened) gain of the Church of God, and could she be blamed if she reported our affairs with less than open sympathy?

Of course the press likes a clerical scandal, and there are certainly journalists who will either paint the least favourable picture they can of the Church and its servants or else take a less than professional pride in the accuracy of their reports. More is the pity that the clergy so often make enemies of potential friends in the media, breaking down relationships which, if built up, would create mutual trust to the benefit of both of the Church and its message and of the journalists who report it. I digress!

It was a holiday disaster which turned up to bring me to a theological transformation, and also introduced me to a contentious issue in which I was to play a major role.

In the summer of 1958, during my Notting Dale curacy, I had – poor as I was – somehow amassed enough wealth to go abroad for my holidays. I had gained a taste for foreign travel while at school, with a sixth-form trip to Paris, five weeks in Burgundy with a pen-friend, and a three-week visit to Malta with the Air Training Corps, outward bound via Gibraltar by destroyer, and returning by air. I felt the urge to go again, and discovered an advertisement for a two-week holiday in Austria for only £23 – 'with Christian fellowship'. I was not too sure of this latter attraction: some fellow-believers can be more than tiresome. Indeed, when I returned I swore I would never take such a holiday again.

We arrived, after a long train journey, in a village on the outskirts of Salzburg, late on the Saturday night. The next morning I went off early into the city to attend High Mass at the cathedral. It was a glorious occasion, with the packed baroque church echoing the heavenly beauty of a Mozart Mass with choir and orchestra.

I arrived back at the hotel just in time for lunch. Where had I been? To church. Was there a Protestant church? No, I'd been to Mass at the Roman Catholic cathedral. There was dead silence. Then someone, speaking for the assembled group, expressed horror that I – a Christian minister too – had been flirting with the Scarlet Woman of Rome. There was no answer to that, beyond a comment that at least I had been to church.

I blotted my copybook even further in the afternoon, when we went for a walk in the village. I went into a café-bar and ordered a Coca-Cola. How could I – a Christian minister at that – drink Coca-Cola when everyone knew it was a drink designed to give young people a taste for alcohol? So it continued throughout an endless two weeks.

On the final evening – after our 'prayer-time' (when in veiled terms it was usually I who was prayed for) – we sat around the table. 'Look what I've bought,' one said, showing an expensive camera; and another, with jewellery. 'You'll have a lot of duty to pay at customs,' said I innocently. 'But we aren't declaring it!' We went round the table, and with the exception of two other fellow-sufferers and myself, every member of the party was intending to cheat the customs. 'I have had your religion up to here the entire holiday,' I said angrily to the company. 'The three of us have been criticised for our faith, treated as less than Christian, our conversion prayed for. And now I find that I have been living in a den of thieves. And hypocrites to boot. Never again!'

The following summer, I determined not to make the same mistake again and decided I would like to go to Sweden. Fr Hugh, a Franciscan who had been a student with me at Chichester, had developed links with the Church of Sweden, and I asked him if he knew of anyone who might like to have an exchange holiday. I soon heard from Pastor Sven-Oscar Berglund, who was then warden of a student's hostel, *Laurentiistiftelsen* in Lund, who invited me to join them at their summer cottage for two weeks if their eldest son, Svante, could return with me.

So began a friendship which has survived more than thirty years, and now spans three generations, with my own son a friend of Sven's grandson, Björn. But it was a small incident which had two much more profound effects on my faith. On a visit to Lund I had a brief meeting with retired bishop, Gustav Aulén. While at college I had dipped into his book on the atonement, *Christus Victor*, and I decided now that I ought to read it properly. Nothing has had so great and immediate an effect on my faith.

In it he sets out three views of the atonement. The first, which he calls the objective or catholic view, sees the sacrifice of Christ in the terms of Mrs Alexander's Good Friday hymn: 'There was no other good enough to pay the price of sin.' This, he suggests, is inadequate, as is the subjective or liberal protestant view that Jesus is simply the example for us to follow, so that as we become like him so we come nearer to God's purpose for us. It is only in the third view, which he calls the classical – and not surprisingly the Lutheran – that the truth is to be found.

I pondered this. Certainly I had never felt the liberal protestant view to be at all satisfactory. But sermons on the substitution view of the atonement I had certainly preached. And I had always believed that when I fell into sin, I must, with God's grace to help me, try, try and try again.

Now I saw in a sudden blinding flash that this was totally inadequate. 'By grace you are saved, through faith: it is the gift of God!' God accepts me as I am, warts and all, for that is the nature of the love of Him who is Love itself. He accepts the inadequacy of my penitence just as he accepts the weakness of my faith. I do not have to earn his love or his grace by working my way into his favour. All that is required of me is to put my trust in his love, to say, 'Help me, for I cannot manage on my own – the journey is too great for me.' Then, and only then, is he able to lift me up into the joy of his presence and glory; my sins are not merely forgiven but wiped off the record, and I can, in St Paul's marvellous words, be 'filled with all the fullness of God'. It transformed my Christian experience, so that the doctrine of justification by faith became, with the conviction that in the Blessed Sacrament of Holy Communion one meets and receives the Real Presence of Jesus, one of the twin pillars of my life in Christ – the one strongly catholic and other strongly protestant.

But it was on this first visit to Sweden that I encountered a problem which was to come more and more to the fore as the years went by: women priests. In 1957, the Swedish Church Assembly had rejected a proposal to allow women to be ordained to the priesthood, and as a result the State had ordered, in true democratic fashion, the Assembly's dissolution and a new election.

Sweden's churchgoer population is minute – about three per cent of the population – but the folk church concept is enshrined in the constitution. A parish church's electoral roll includes all those on the secular electoral list who have not opted out as members of another Church. Thus the election to the parochial church council is held on party lines, and a PCC may well include a majority who never attend church services. The 1957/8 Church Assembly election was fought on the issue of women priests – as a matter of justice rather than as a theological issue – and party politics dominated the result.

The new Assembly meekly accepted the requirement to pass legislation to allow women to be priests, and the first were ordained in 1960. Those who opposed were pilloried in the media and generally held up to public ridicule. Priests who remained opposed, men of high calibre like Pastor Berglund – godly, scholarly, and without question *episcopabile* – were isolated and began to find it difficult to be appointed to parishes. Only one bishop was appointed after 1960 who opposed the ordination of women, Bertil Gärtner of Göteborg, and then only because the diocese put forward three names, all of whom were in opposition.

Some years later, his predecessor, Bishop Bo Giertz, told me that Gärtner's attitude had led to him receiving death threats and to his children being mistreated at school. 'He is,' Giertz told me, 'a confessor for the faith and has suffered greatly.'

I began to see that, whatever the superficial attraction of arguments in favour of women's ordination, there was an underlying element which was, to say the least, not of God. St Paul described 'emnity, strife, dissension, party-spirit' as 'works of the flesh', which he contrasted with the fruits of the Spirit. Many women coming forward to seek ordination are sincere, godly and able, and if we oppose the ordination we must see to what ministry God is calling them if, as we believe, it is not to the priesthood. Part of their undoubted pain must be to witness some of their number disseminating that which so clearly emerges as the works of the flesh. At its more subtle level, it manifests itself as a blanket dismissal of opponents as psychologically disordered, guided by fear, misogynist, homosexual, sexually repressed, power-hungry, to be pitied by the liberated. More crudely, it becomes an aggressive determination to 'get rid of them'. One English woman, interviewed immediately after her ordination in the United States, was asked if her action might cause some to leave the Church of England. 'Good riddance if they do!' was her reply.

In 1989, on a visit to Canada to listen to groups representing all points of view, I had in one diocese priests coming to me secretly by night with sealed envelopes: 'Read that, but for goodness sake don't make public my name – I have my wife and family to think of!' They feared, not violence but dismissal.

Even in England, there have been many deplorable incidents. One priest, after speaking in his diocesan synod debate against women in the priesthood, had a telephone call two days later from a member of his diocesan bishop's senior staff. He was told bleakly that his career was finished in that diocese and he might as well find a job somewhere else. Just before a major debate in the General Synod, I was myself warned that a meeting had been held by supporters of the issue to brief a senior member of Synod to make a personal attack on me. Opponents have certainly held briefing meetings before debates to ensure that those taking part will cover all sides of the argument against, but never to my knowledge – and I would know if it were otherwise – has anyone been briefed in the unchristian art of the personal attack.

There are many theological arguments against the ordination of women to the priesthood, and a major problem of acceptable Christian debate on this issue is that both sides can follow the same path almost to end of the debate and then come to an opposite and incompatible conclusion. For example, we can both agree that the glory of God's creation is its diversity, and argue that this diversity must therefore be reflected in the ministry. One will say that therefore both men and women must be admitted to the same priesthood, whereas the other will say that, no, the diversity cannot be in the sex of the priest but in the form of ministry and that a different kind of ministry must be exercised by women – for instance in a reformed diaconate. In the same way we can agree that the priest at the altar represents Jesus Christ – but in his maleness or in his humanity? We can agree that for those who are in Christ there is neither male nor female – but in similarity or distinctiveness?

I believe that God calls no one to that which is impossible, and since I believe it is impossible for a woman to be ordained priest, I must reject the vocations of those women who seek to be priests, and that must be painful for them. And since I dare not deny that God may have called them to full-time ministry, it is a requirement for me that I support the search for a women's ministry which is equal to that of the man but different in kind, more than likely a renewed and reformed diaconate.

But even more painful for women who seek ordination is the knowledge that, however firm they are in a traditional faith, however much they hold to biblical standards, they depend for their support on many for whom the ordination is only a rather more visible part of a liberal package to which they are otherwise totally opposed – a package which includes homosexual liberation and the acceptance of single-sex 'marriage' along with the abandonment of other aspects of Christian and scriptural ethics; the adoption of feminist concepts which will fundamentally change the doctrine of God and allow him to be addressed as Mother and Daughter instead of Father and Son; a general diminution of the concept of sin and with it the idea of Christ as the individual's redeemer; and the gradual adoption of pagan New Age theologies.

What would be left would bear little relation to the Christian faith, and with this emerging at the beginning of a Decade of Evangelism, I can do no other than regard it as not merely an aberration but as a powerful irruption of Evil in the life of the Church world-wide. Little wonder, then, that wherever – Sweden, the United States, Canada, New Zealand and now Britain – the issue of women in the priesthood has emerged, so too have Paul's works of the flesh: emnity, strife, bitterness, dissension, party-spirit. Our fight against women in the priesthood is not an attack on good, godly, sincere Christian women – for they are all of that – but part of the continuing battle against the onslaught of the powers and principalities of the darkness of this world. And sometimes against spiritual wickedness in very high places indeed.

Little could I have known when I asked Fr Hugh if he knew of someone who would like an exchange holiday, or when I first met Sven-Oscar Berglund on the railway station at Lund and struck up an immediate friendship, that God was signing me up for a task through which I would have a small part to play in the battle for the soul of the church which is his body.

Had I known, I would have known too not to fear, for there would be the sure protection of the shield of faith, the helmet of salvation and the sword of the Spirit which is the word of God. For whatever the pains we must suffer in the battles he calls us to fight, the war itself has already been won on the Cross.

Chapter seven

Chaplain and Vicar

Rosamund Essex's visit on that mid-week afternoon in Notting Dale did more than launch me on a very minor journalistic career – though it did that, and I have been thankful for the challenges it has brought, not least in the discipline which sometimes demands articles of a thousand words at a couple of hours' notice. The fact that my first article for the *Church Times* was quickly followed by another, on youth work, was the probable cause of my name coming to the notice of Prebendary Gordon Philips, the brilliant but erratic senior Anglican chaplain to the University of London.

David Scott (later to be Archdeacon of Stow) was leaving, and to my surprise Gordon wrote to ask if I would be interested in succeeding him. I already knew Ivor Smith-Cameron, who was chaplain to the West London colleges, and had given a couple of talks to his students. And the Bishop of Kensington, Cyril East-augh, was chairman of the chaplaincy council. I felt it was time to be leaving Notting Dale, so I talked to each of them and quickly accepted Gordon's offer.

I was to live in the East End and minister particularly in the London School of Economics and Queen Mary College, but also in the various medical schools – at the London, Charing Cross, St Mary's, Royal Free, and Royal Dental Hospitals. In addition, I was to be chaplain to the two university church choirs, one of students and the other a boys' choir which sang at Sunday morning Mattins, with boys from Latymer Upper School where the director of music, John Poole, was a master.

It was a tall order and I enjoyed every minute of it. I lodged first in a vicarage room in Coburn Road, Stepney and then, after

79

three months, in the attic of All Hallows Rectory, Bow, spending about three hours a day driving in London traffic and gaining an encyclopaedic knowledge of the by-ways of London's East End.

All our work was centred on the Eucharist, which I celebrated during the week in lecture rooms in QMC and LSE, in hospital chapels, and sometimes in student rooms, with an informality greatly contrasting with the music and liturgy at St George's, Bloomsbury, one of Hawksmoor's gems and at that time the university church. Some fifteen years later, when attending a deanery clergy chapter Eucharist in a school, I protested at the chaplain's informality (the call to receive communion was 'There's plenty of wine so have a good swig!'), I was thought, not for the first time nor the last, to be a reactionary fuddy-duddy. I remembered wryly that I had rejoiced at greater informality all those years before. But we never confused informality with irreverence.

There were midday meetings to organise, study groups to attend, students to counsel, confessions to hear, on a patch which took me from central London to the Student hostels in Woodford, some fifteen miles to the east. And because I seemed to pick up engagements which others could not cover, I would sometimes trek out as far as Royal Holloway College in the west beyond Heathrow.

On Sundays, I would celebrate the Eucharist at 8 a.m. at Westfield College, which I enjoyed but which for some reason others did not; then back to a packed Sung Eucharist at St George's followed by an immaculately sung service of Matins with a tiny congregation from its former use as a parish church. And in the evening, the church would bulge at the seams for Evensong and the university sermon, to which the leading churchmen of the day were glad to be invited as guest preacher – though none surpassed Gordon Phillips himself.

The team was a mixed bunch. Welcoming me at my first chaplaincy council, Gordon said it was now the best team he had ever had, but I was quickly to learn that he was a man of enthusiasms. The Rectory in Gower Street was large enough for a bachelor to let out rooms, and this he did to a stream of students. Each new arrival had a 'brilliant mind' and 'promised to be one of the best students of his year'. After only a few weeks they would fall from grace: 'a great disappointment – he'll have to go'. And go he quickly did, to be replaced with a star of even greater magnitude.

Gordon did in fact have a genius for identifying able students with quick minds. But he wanted a passive audience against which to bounce his ideas, and able students with quick minds were wont to answer back as soon as they gained sufficient confidence in the relationship. Gordon could never cope with this, and so out they went, often hurt and bewildered.

The most able of the team was undoubtedly Ivor Smith-Cameron, who had an affinity with young people which could not be matched. Those who know him now as the exotically-clad full-of-eastern-promise radical Canon Missioner of Southwark will find it hard to visualise Ivor as always be-cassocked, and conservative in all (or at least most) of his ways. He survived because he was able, by living and working entirely in the West London area, to follow on his own account the advice which he gave me: to keep out of Gordon's way or face dismissal or a nervous breakdown.

That option was not open to me because I had to have an office in the Gower Street rectory. Nor was it in my nature to obey the other, less creditable, commandments necessary for a safe passage: thou shalt not disagree with any view Gordon expresses; thou shalt not challenge any idea he puts forward; and above all else, thou shalt not dissent when those around you cease to be flavour of the month.

I preached the university sermon on the feast of Pentecost and was summoned to his study the next day. He dissected what I had said, commented at length and helpfully, and gave me the verbal equivalent of eight out of ten, which was praise indeed. I ought to have recognised the warning signs.

He went on: 'But I want to tell you that you are not happy here.' I said I was perfectly happy. 'No, you are not,' he countered, 'and you will have to leave.' It was a bombshell, though had I been less naïve I should have picked up the warnings: silences when I discussed future plans with other staff members, conversations ending when I appeared on the scene, knowing smiles. When must I leave? 'Oh, at the end of the next academic year – in twelve months.' Very odd, I thought, but I supposed he wanted to get it off his chest.

Then on the day before term began in September I was again summoned to his study. 'You are to leave,' he told me. I replied that I knew that I was to leave as he had already told me – at the end of the academic year the following June. 'No, you are to leave now – today!'

I was angry. The only clergy who leave like that are those who have been in trouble with small boys or sleeping with girls, and I certainly had no intention of leaving with a totally unjustifiable cloud of that kind hanging over me. The Bishop of Kensington gave me his full support and Gordon backed down, saying – with accuracy – that my programme for that term was so full that it could not possibly be covered with a member of staff short.

Gordon melted then and said he knew everyone in the Church of England (which he did) and that he would give me every assistance (which he did not) in finding a new post. I had begun to doubt his omniscience after he had proudly told the staff meeting, when the see of Canterbury was vacant, that he had been busy all day successfully blocking the appointment of Michael Ramsey. The very next day it was announced that Michael Ramsey was to be the 100th Archbishop of Canterbury.

In fact, though I enjoyed my short spell as a university chaplain, I suspect Gordon was right that I was ill-equipped for the work. I am not an innovator and am uneasy when required to create the task rather than fulfilling a task already there – in modern jargon I am at my best when I can be reactive and at my worst when I must be proactive. Nevertheless my time there was part of God's plan for me, and it was certainly a year when I was forced to use parts of the brain which had been untaxed in Chorley or Notting Dale.

There was the privilege, too, of seeing young Christians suddenly finding faith. One young man turned up at a college mid-week Eucharist, took communion and at breakfast afterwards, said, 'That was nice – what was it?' He was prepared for baptism and confirmation and is now ordained.

In fact the chaplaincy was a great source of vocations to the priesthood. I was not there long enough to claim any credit, but years earlier when I was browsing through the books in my library, I found one which had been given to me by the students of Queen Mary College when I left. A third of those men are now priests.

But as that autumn progressed, the need to find another job pressed upon me. Two London posts were put my way – one in Shepherd's Bush, a stone's throw from Notting Dale (I had asked for something different and it wasn't!), and one in the East End. The Bishop of Stepney saw me at lunch one day in Queen Mary College and came over to me. 'I can't tell you why, but don't go,' he said. A few weeks later the vicar was arrested.

By now it was mid-November and in six weeks I would be homeless and jobless. Somehow I was put in touch with the Bishop of St Albans, Michael Gresford-Jones. The first possibility foundered when the vicar's main concern when interviewing me seemed to be whether or not I could move chairs. Then I went to see Canon Christopher Mackonochie, the rector of Dunstable. All fell into place, and it was immediately clear that this was the job I was meant to have. I spent the next twenty-seven years in that diocese, in three parishes. I joined the staff of Dunstable Priory on New Year's Day, 1961, for what was probably the most important four-year period of my life, both as an individual and as a priest.

As well as the rector, there were to be three curates – Robert Butler, who was in charge of one of the daughter churches, St

Augustine's; Rupert Child, who came later in that same year; and myself, to be mainly at the Priory. Rupert Child was to have particular responsibility for Christ Church (then technically part of the parish of Houghton Regis) and to develop a new site for a daughter church to be dedicated to St Fremund, an obscure saint whose cult the Augustinians had attempted to promote in the middle ages, in order to rival the rich shrine of St Alban a few miles to the south (and to pay for the frequent and financially crippling visits of king and courtiers).

We met daily for Mattins at 7 a.m., Mass at 7.30 a.m. and Evensong at 5 p.m., and on most days we were joined by lay members of the congregation. At the weekly staff meeting, we shared out the visiting, though the two curates with their own centres of worship tended to cover their own areas while the rector and I did the remainder. It shared the work fairly and for me emphasised the value of visiting – that you come to be known and trusted through social visiting so that you are known and trusted when crises arise.

But in a parish of 25,000 people four priests had plenty to occupy them besides social visiting – hospital calls, sick communions, eighty weddings a year, baptisms in abundance, funerals, classes to teach in the church school, study groups, confirmation groups. Canon Mackonochie knew how to delegate and would leave us to our own devices without the interference which marks a lack of trust. I soon found myself secretary of the local Council of Churches, and then was its chairman for a year – not every rector would allow his curate such latitude and responsibility. And at one period, I was governor of thirteen schools, junior, secondary, grammar, and comprehensive.

Once again the choir became a particular concern. The rector was keen to develop the quality (already very high) of church music at the Priory, and persuaded the parochial church council that this would mean paying a higher-than-usual salary to the organist and choirmaster. This was agreed, and I suggested I might contact Christopher Scarf, then sub-organist at Ely Cathedral.

84

Christopher had been at school with John Poole, the director of music at the university chaplaincy, who had invited him to join a choir visit to Sweden. He was an outstanding young musician and – a little to my surprise and much to my delight – he agreed to come. He became head of music at a local school and this at once provided an additional source of choirboys. Like all good choirboys, they were unruly, boisterous, full of mischief, but under Chris Scarf's tuition they sang like angels. Not only were people brought to the glory and mystery of God by the beauty of musical offering, but boys and young men began to have a glimpse of God's call to full-time service.

Of those boys of the class of 1961–4, Vic Goodman, Martin Baldock, Graeme Knowles and John Hayward are ordained and Colin Hudspith is in training as a late ordinand; Bob Harwood is a church organist; and David Cheetham (a server) a diocesan registrar. Anona Maskell (a choirman's daughter) is a churchwarden, and school friends of the choir realised that it was nothing too odd to want to become a priest. Several of them are now ordained, both in the Church of England and in the Roman Catholic Church.

No group ever works together without disagreements, and occasionally at staff meetings these would flare up into arguments. But Christopher was in every way a good leader and a good boss, easily smoothing ruffled feathers, strong and sure enough to accept opposition, and never bearing grudges. It was in every way a happy four years.

Christopher Mackonochie trusted us to cope with the most serious tragedies, and that in itself was a confidence-booster. At eight o'clock one cold morning, I had to call on a mother and father and sit with them as their son was executed in Bedford Prison. I had long been opposed to capital punishment but that experience ensured that my views would never change. As I read prayers from the Burial Office, I felt the hypocrisy of a member of a society on whose behalf a man's life was being taken, coldly and deliberately. And I knew the truth of Archbishop William

Temple's argument that society should so abhor the taking of a life that it should not itself take a murderer's life.

One event above all in Dunstable changed my life totally, and totally for the better. It was the custom to hold a parish Christmas Party in the old Dunstable Town Hall, now demolished, and in 1961 I was asked to organise the entertainment. An old college friend, Dennis King, was then curate at St Peter's, Luton, and so I asked him if he would come over and do a 'turn'. He agreed on condition that he could bring a 'beautiful blonde'.

The beautiful blonde turned out to be a teacher from an infants' school in Stopsley, Roberta Thompson, known to all as Bobbie. I was smitten – completely, absolutely and irrevocably and, having wormed out of Dennis that she was just a friend, called at her school after an afternoon visit to the nearby crematorium – clergy combine romance with unusual activities.

Bobbie came over to Dunstable for a meal on the Sunday after I had returned from my Christmas break, we met for lunch on the Thursday, and the following Saturday met again in London (where I had joined my father in the afternoon for a visit by Bury FC to play Charlton Athletic at the Dell) and went to the theatre. I had left my car in the car park at High Barnet underground station, surely one of the most unromantic spots in north London. I realised that if I felt as I did when we returned there to drive home it must be love, and so I proposed – six days after our first date. Bobbie, to my surprise and delight, said yes.

We were married six months later on Saturday 21st July 1962, in a splendid ceremony in Dunstable Priory. Christopher married us and Dennis was best man and then celebrant at the nuptial Mass. The choir excelled themselves, with the highlights a setting of Psalm 122, *I was glad when they said unto me*, written by Chris Scarf, the haunting O *Mysterium Ineffabile* by Lallouette as the communion motet, and singing the mass to the *Missa de Angelis*. For our honeymoon, we flew to Sweden where Sven-Oscar Berglund had lent us his summer cottage at Vikhög on the southern coast opposite Copenhagen.

We continued to live in the rectory flat in West Street, Dunstable, and worked at being married. Over the years that have followed we have had our differences and rows, always keeping one special rule: that when this happened we would never go to sleep or leave for work without settling the argument. It worked: it must have done, for now after thirty years together we still hold hands of an evening as we watch television, and we are each other's best friend.

I was already thirty years old when we met, so Bobbie was not the first serious girlfriend I had had, nor the first I thought I might marry. Some became dear friends, but the sparkle that happened when Bobbie and I first met was not there. Others might one day have become lovers but never could have become friends. And how many marriages must have failed with those ingredients? I thank God for Bobbie, but I thank him too for the grace and strength which prevented me causing misery to more than one life by a foolish marriage.

Marriage taught me much about God, and gave flesh to the cold bare bones of my deepening awareness and doctrine of justification – that it is by grace that we are saved, through faith, and that this is the free gift of God. Married love must see the partner as he or she is, loving not just the lovable, nor even in spite of the unlovable. In Elizabeth Barrett Browning's words, love can be 'for naught except for love's sake only', freely given, freely accepted and freely accepting, warts and all. If that is true of human love how much more must it be true to God who is Love itself?

My prayer life, too, gained a new reality. With its centre the Eucharist and nurtured by a regular and unfailing recitation of the daily office, alone or more usually with others, I had found Scripture and the Psalms a constant source of renewal of my faith and understanding. But the setting aside of a fixed period daily for particular intercessions always seemed to have within it something inherently artificial, as if God's love and care for those for whom I prayed depended – which I knew it did not – on the spinning of my imaginary prayer wheel for fifteen minutes a day.

But prayer is not a mechanical exercise. Rather it is a relationship. Similarly my relationship with Bobbie did not require me to set aside fifteen minutes a day for conversation, advice and requests. In fact nothing could have been more certain to damage our developing bond. One priest I know used to call his four children to his study every day at six o'clock in the evening. Each would be asked about their day, be patted on their head by their doting father and sent on their way. A loving relationship? Surely not!

Yet another priest saw one evening from his diary that someone had an appointment to see him at 9.45 p.m. His wife knocked at his study door and he apologised that he couldn't speak to her as he was expecting a visitor. 'The visitor is me,' said his wife. 'I knew that the only way we could have a conversation together would be if I made an appointment in your diary.'

But married love is, like prayer, a relationship – constant, ever-present, as much in silence as in conversation, content and secure in the other's presence, caring and understanding at all times, knowing needs before the need to ask. It was the writer of the medieval spiritual classic, *The Cloud of Unknowing*, who said that God 'does not ask for help, he asks for you'. That is at the heart of true marriage as it is at the heart of true prayer.

By 1964, it was clear that the time was coming for me to move. I had been nine years in orders, long even for those days without my own parish. After one or two false starts, the Bishop of St Albans suggested I should look at Eaton Bray, a village about three miles from Dunstable, where the vicar, Peter Graham, was leaving to become rector of Harpenden. Although it was near to Dunstable, it was a different kind of community, centred on farming rather than the car industry. Bobbie was by now teaching at the Ashton School in Dunstable and would be able to continue with her career, which was an important consideration. I knew the church and vicarage, and met the churchwardens as prospective incumbent. We liked each other, the Bishop made the formal offer, and I accepted.

Parting from friends in a parish is always a bereavement and we had made many friends in Dunstable. But we were not to be far away, and it is easier for an ex-curate to continue friendships from a nearby parish than it is for a vicar, for the courtesy of avoiding stepping on the toes of the vicar who succeeds him is not demanded. And some, like Dr Sam Twivy and his wife, Sheila, remain close friends.

The worship at the Priory had been for us the Church of England at its best. At our farewell, the mass was to the *Missa de Angelis* and the choir sang once again Lallouette's *O Mysterium Ineffabile* as the communion motet. Bobbie cried all the way to the altar and I too was not far from tears.

My induction was on September 15th 1964, and I have a photograph taken in the vestry of Eaton Bray church. The Bishop looks benign, the diocesan secretary, Evelyn Busby, looks formidable in her cloche hat, the Rural Dean looks relieved and I look just simply nervous.

It was good to have my own parish but lonely without the companionship of a large staff. The church building was a delight – thirteenth-century and unspoiled, with a characteristic 'Hertfordshire spike' (a small spire added to a tower), ironwork by Thomas de Leighton on the south door, and an interior of great beauty.

We lived in the sort of old and over-large vicarage that archdeacons in the 1960s rejoiced to replace with unsuitable and inadequate boxes, which archdeacons in the 1990s find require more expenditure in upkeep than those old and over-large vicarages which survived archidiaconal vandalism. It was partly Georgian with Victorian extensions, surrounding an older farmhouse kitchen. There were seven bedrooms, mostly large, and with the help of B bbie's parents and uncle, we set about decorating and making it a home. Had Bobbie not been teaching, we should have found it difficult financially, though I was now on the princely stipend of £1,000 a year (about £8,220 at 1990 values, considerably less than the 1990 incumbent's inadequate stipend of £11,800).

The house was surrounded by a garden of two-and-a-half acres, with a lake and a wild area. It took me the whole of a day off to mow the front lawn and cut the grass in the orchard behind the house, and after a time we employed a lad from the village to do it as a Saturday job. A hundred years before, a gardener-vicar had planned it carefully and the trees which greeted us as we opened the front door were a delightful pattern of varying greens and russet-browns. Beyond the orchard was a vegetable patch, let out to the organist's husband. It was rent free, but from time to time we would find a huge bag of fresh-picked peas or beans or lettuce by the back door. By the vegetable patch was a muddy area beyond the lake, where at Christmas we twice had to bury a too-dead capon, presented to us by a grateful parishioner.

Two widowed sisters lived at the farm next door to us, daughters of the founder of the nurseries which still gave employment and tied cottages to many of the villagers. Each called on us and each left cheques of £50 towards carpets and curtains, hinting that more would follow, especially at Christmas and Easter. We were grateful for their kindness.

But in the village we found we were piggy-in-the-middle. There were those who regarded themselves as the gentry and had sherry together every Sunday morning after church to which their 'equals' were invited. We were not. Other village families who had been used to doffing their caps to 'the vicarage' excluded us too. We were neither 'one of us' nor 'one of them' – all the more disconcerting since neither of us cared a fig for such distinctions anyway.

We gradually broke down the village barriers, for they found we were not the sort who expected caps to be doffed. The Methodists were particularly kind to us. They were a strong congregation, made all the stronger by those for whom it was a way of silent protest against others who were – so it seemed to them – 'the Church'. We used the vicarage dining room as a parish meeting room and Bobbie (who has never been or aspired to be a 'typical' vicar's wife) ran a hugely successful Young Wives Group and made many friends. Some we still see, and when we do time seems to have stood still.

The first two years were hard, harder than I could have expected and for reasons to which my eyes were gradually opened. I was never one to force change on an unwilling church, though any new vicar brings his own ideas to meet the changing needs of a congregation. Mine were modest and not disruptive of the accepted pattern of the parish.

One need, I perceived, was to provide a children's service and, tentatively, I put the suggestion that it would be good to have Junior Church service at 10.30 a.m. in between the Sung Eucharist at 9 a.m. and 11.30 Mattins. No one would be inconvenienced and the growing number of children would be taught the Christian faith in the context of worship. It was resisted valiantly but ultimately unsuccessfully. I knew it was the right thing to introduce, though apprehensive since I was aware that I was not good with that age group of children. I found, of course – as I have always found when one follows the course of action which God has indicated – that I was given the necessary skills to complete the task.

We wanted the Sung Eucharist to become a family service, but as much as I persuaded those with young children to attend, they were dissuaded by hints and pressures from others. One young mum brought her baby after much hesitation, only to be told on her first Sunday, 'We don't like babies at our service, dear!'

I happened to meet the Bishop's wife some months after my induction. 'Eaton Bray?' she said. 'A very stony corner of the Lord's vineyard, that!' She was right, but it was not quite what her husband had said when he inducted me.

What was wrong? Perhaps it was me, I wondered. I looked round the congregation one Sunday. They were all good people and many were very nice, kind, friendly folk. Yet somehow everything was undermined in a subtle and almost sinister way.

It was Bobbie who inadvertently gave me the clue. We were returning from an Easter break, and as we drove into the village she was pensive. What was the matter? 'Well,' she replied, 'it's as if there's a black cloud of evil overhanging this place.' I am not one who sees evil spirits in anything that upsets my pet desires, but I was disturbed by what she had said. For there *was* something desperately wrong. I told the Bishop of Bedford, John Hare, a good and holy man, but down-to-earth too and a man of great experience. 'Doesn't surprise me at all,' he said cheerily. 'There's a swathe of it cutting right through Bedfordshire. Didn't know it stretched as far as you.'

We had a large, thick ledger, hand-written, as the minute-book of the parochial church council, recording meetings right back to the early 1920s when PCCs first came into being. The Annual Church Meeting was approaching and I decided to examine the minutes of every PCC meeting over those forty years. I found that every time a vicar, a bishop – anyone – had suggested something for the renewal of the church and the spread of the gospel, it had been either resisted, rejected or simply defied. So I listed every occasion, carefully and methodically, and read it out as my annual report to the parish. Throughout my speech, one parishioner held a metal ash-tray and banged it rhythmically on the tiled window-sill of the hall. I thought I might be lynched, but after I had finished there was a deathly hush and the meeting ended quickly and quietly.

A little later, in a parish magazine article, I wrote about a Christian's attitude to politics, suggesting (as I have always done since) that a Christian ought to bring a Christian attitude to every part of life, including political views, always giving primacy to the demands of Jesus Christ.

There was a terrible explosion in each case, but the pattern was broken. I had little notes of thanks and support, and unexpected people stopped me in the street to congratulate me for saying what I had said. And although there were those who disapproved of what I had said and done, no one left the church, and there was no emnity between us. Today, on the rare occasions that I meet even the most fervent of my opponents, we meet with the warmth of long friendship.

In a most remarkable way, an unhappy parish became happy, and the black cloud lifted. And a rather unspiritual priest realised with a flash of insight that evil is not the absence of good, as he had believed, but a power to be reckoned with – and to be met without fear. They *were* good people, but sometimes we do indeed 'fight not against flesh and blood but against the principalities and powers of the darkness of this world'. It was a lesson I have had cause to remember on more than one occasion in the years that have followed.

There was joy and gratitude in our family life. For the years in Eaton Bray saw two important additions to our family. In December 1968, we saw an advertisement in the *Times* for dalmatian puppies. We had wanted a dog and drove down to Ripley in Surrey, where in a converted water-mill fifteen puppies had been born to a splendid bitch. We had thought we would have a dog but there were only two in the litter, both believed to be deaf. I thought all of them were gorgeous, but Bobbie kept picking out one which the owner insisted she was keeping for breeding.

In the event, the choice was not to be ours at all. For one puppy kept pushing its way to the front of the seething mass of polka-dotted fur, insisting that she was the one who had decided that we should be the lucky ones. Her Kennel Club name (for she had aristocratic forebears in the shape of national and international champions) was Cerbera Lucinda. Cerberus was the hound who guarded the gates of Hell. For everyday use, she was Lucy (and more often just simply 'Our Loo'). It was Bishop John Trillo, then of Hertford, who on a visit soon afterwards pointed out to us that Lucy was the name of the Bishop of St Albans' wife. We genuinely had no idea.

Lucy was a great joy to us, loving, loyal, mischievous, vain (she was an elegant dog and revelled in being told so), intelligent, enthusiastic, boisterous, and when some eleven years later I had to take her to be put down, it was the greatest grief of my life. I know it would not compare to the sadness of losing a wife or child, but it was a deep bereavement from which I took long to recover. Perhaps there was the added uncertainty about the future. A human being dies, and there is grief and loss and emptiness. But there is the certain hope of eternal life and a reunion which will then never be broken. But a dog? However close, however much a friend, however loved and loving? Who can know? Yet if this life is a preparation for the next, it must surely bear some resemblance to it, and, for many of us, the love of animals is an important part of this life. I do not have remotely the same certainty about this that I hold about the resurrection of the body, but I suspect that, when I die, Lucy will be with those who greet me, tail wagging furiously and lips curled in that 'smile' she saved for special occasions.

There was a strange sequel to her death. I went to the vet's surgery in Stanmore well before nine o'clock when it was due to open, in order to be the first in line. I knew I should weep and had seen on other occasions the embarrassment of owners at such a time. The deed done, I came home and could say nothing at all to the family about it.

About three months later, over breakfast, Bobbie recounted a dream she had had that night. She was driving along a country road and saw a dalmatian dog lying on a grassy bank by the roadside. It was injured and unconscious, its legs twitching and its tongue peeping through its parted lips. She saw my face and said immediately, 'It's all right, it wasn't Lucy.' 'How was she lying in relation to you?' I asked. She told me, carefully and gently. 'Well,' I said, 'that was precisely my last sight of Lucy.' 'But this dog was wet through.' 'What you didn't know, because I couldn't tell you, was that as we waited at the surgery door for the vet to open up, it was pouring with rain and poor Lucy was soaked to the skin. And then afterwards, I drove home the country way because there would be less traffic.'

Coincidence, or did something pass between the minds of two people joined in love?

Just over a year after Lucy joined the family, Bobbie gave birth to our only child, Jeremy, and our family was complete. In those days, it was more common for births to take place in the home and we had arranged that this would be the case. Dr Twivy enjoyed caring for pregnancies and was an attentive friend.

For comfort's sake, Bobbie had been sleeping in a spare bedroom, and when the waters broke had difficulty in rousing me. I called her parents, living some eight miles away in Luton, and her mother promised to come over as arranged. We informed the midwife and there seemed no cause for urgency. Four hours later, still no one had arrived. From movies I knew that hot water came into it somewhere, and I wondered what I was supposed to do with it. I rang the midwife again, who patronised what she thought was an over-anxious pregnant father. 'Stop panicking, and call me again when the contractions are coming every ten minutes, dear,' she counselled. 'But they're coming every five minutes.' There was a moment's silence. 'I'll be along at once.' And she was.

The doctor arrived and I paced up and down in the kitchen making endless cups of coffee. Lucy stood beneath our bedroom window and howled. Mother-in-law eventually arrived, somewhat fraught. Outside a new drain was being laid, and the local authority chose that very day to complete the task and to turn off the mains water.

It had looked like being an easy birth, but I began to pick up signs that all was not well. At one o'clock, Sam Twivy rang for an ambulance, explaining that the baby was round the wrong way and showing signs of distress. The ambulance manoeuvred around the road-works and just about managed to enter the vicarage drive. Bobbie was put on board and I followed by car. Then at the bottom of Totternhoe Hill, the blue light and siren went on and I followed precariously as we skirted traffic lights, overtook cars and sped to Luton Maternity Hospital, where a perfect baby boy was safely delivered.

It was 2.20 p.m. on 31st January 1969. It was only when I had sent out all the birth announcement cards for a Patrick Giles that we decided he was really Jeremy Paul. He has always been a delight and I will not embarrass him in this account by saying more. Perhaps I do not love him more than my own father loved me, though I think I do. But I have tried not to make the mistakes in our relationship that my father made. I suspect I have made my own gaffes, and if he should write an account like this forty years hence, I might learn what they were – though I doubt if I shall reach the age of a hundred. But he is now a journalist and will be a better writer than I shall ever be. It would be a good read.

Jeremy was only a few months old when it became clear that it was time to move. At Easter 1970, I was asked to look at St Peter's, Bushey Heath, on the southern edge of the diocese of St Albans and almost in London. I met the churchwardens, Alan Taylor and Brian James, who grilled me for two hours. I liked this – and them – and accepted the Bishop of Hertford's offer, for Michael Gresford-Jones had just retired.

The new Bishop was the principal of Cuddesdon Theological College, Robert Runcie, and he interviewed me in his temporary study in the diocesan conference centre, Verulam House, in St Albans. He said how good it was to meet a priest whose views exactly matched his own.

I should have guessed it would not last.

Chapter eight

Church on the Heath

I was inducted as vicar of St Peter's, Bushey Heath, on St Peter's Day, June 29th 1970, which also happened to be Bobbie's birthday. It was Robert Runcie's first induction service, though the process leading to the appointment had of course been largely completed before he appeared on the scene. Which for my sake was probably just as well.

St Albans was a happy diocese, with a deservedly good reputation for the pastoral care of its clergy under two fine bishops, Michael Furse and Michael Gresford-Jones. But it lacked the sparkle of modern ideas and it was important that new blood should be brought in. This Robert Runcie did, and during his ten years as Bishop only a handful – three at most, I would guess – of senior parishes and posts were given to clergy from the diocese.

When he eventually left to become Archbishop of Canterbury, the outstanding ability of those whom he had brought in was able to be recognised in their appointment as deans and bishops – Alec Graham, Peter Mumford and Bob Hardy went as bishops of Newcastle, Truro and Lincoln; John Simpson, Hugh Dickenson, Kenneth Jennings, Trevor Beeson and Nicholas Coulton became deans of Canterbury, Salisbury, Gloucester, and Winchester and provost of Newcastle; with suffragan sees going to Christopher Mayfield, Richard Llewelin, Michael Scott-Joynt and Keith Arnold.

St Albans had been largely a moderate and theologically orthodox catholic diocese, with few extremes, but the influx of newcomers brought rapid changes. It was unexpected, not least because Dr Runcie had come from Cuddesdon Theological

College where he had been principal throughout the 1960s. Surprising though it may seem to those who today know Cuddesdon as a leading representative of theological liberalism, in 1970 it had retained its catholic reputation, gained during the principalships of Eric Graham (whose son, Peter, I had succeeded at Eaton Bray) and Edward Knapp-Fisher, later Bishop of Pretoria and, later still, tireless in his work for Anglican-Roman Catholic ecumenism.

Gradually the diocese took on a new look, and had we had the insight to be aware of it, there were many hints about the direction in which the Church of England as a whole would slowly be guided, as its establishment became dominated by those brought up in the new theology of the Sixties. As I think back to my early days in St Albans, with its tolerance and comprehensiveness – which were a mirror of the Church of England itself in those days – as well as its catholic worship and theological orthodoxy, it is hard to equate it with the diocese I knew in my latter years. But that is to move ahead too quickly.

As I emerged in procession out of the vestry at my induction, I found a church packed to the doors. My heart turned over and I wondered what I had taken on. In his sermon, Dr Runcie warned the congregation of my obsession with the concept of the ministry of the whole church, and implied – quite correctly – that whatever ministry I had in Bushey Heath I would expect to share with the laity. 'Indeed,' he went on, 'the rural dean of Dunstable tells me that it is hard for a priest to get near the pulpit during the interregnum at Eaton Bray!'

It was quite true. When I first went to the parish, the churchwarden had told me proudly that during that interregnum every service, every lesson, every prayer had been read by an ordained priest – not even a Reader had managed to set foot in the church. When I left, lessons and prayers were taken by lay folk, and even on occasions the address. While I was on holiday, Mattins and Evensong were maintained by the laity, who also conducted some of the Bible studies.

At Bushey Heath, on the contrary, my predecessor Myles Raikes had already begun the process. There was an active baptism preparation group, and never once during my eighteen years as vicar did I need to conduct a baptism class. In fact, I worked on the principle that if I had to do anything which could be done by the lay members of the church, then it was a measure of failure.

Shared leadership is always risky, and sometimes one has to allow things to happen without interference even if one is a mite uneasy. Only once in my eighteen years at Bushey Heath did I restrain a group which had been given responsibility from exercising it as they wished.

Our baptism policy had always been open, so long as certain requirements were fulfilled. The baptism was to be at the main service of the church, in accordance with canon law; the parents were to attend whatever preparation was offered; they were to consider the promises they would be asked to take; and then if they felt they could make those promises in a good conscience, it was not for us to question their integrity. The baptism group came up with a much more rigorist policy, by which, for example, parents who had had a first baby baptised and had not attended church afterwards would be refused. I could not support this and would not allow it. Do that too often, and people will eventually refuse to take on responsibilities; but shared leadership does not mean leadership is abandoned.

It was exciting – and a new experience – to be vicar of a parish where the parochial church council were enthusiastic to try new ideas. For my first few years at Eaton Bray, I had felt that though I would not want a PCC of 'yes-men', even that would be preferable to the one I had of 'no-men'. But at Bushey Heath it was the vicar who sometimes had to be the restraining influence.

While I was at Eaton Bray, the experimental Holy Communion service entered the scene, and I introduced it with all the inborn deviousness of a future archdeacon. The dominant group, centred on the Farm, never attended the Sung Eucharist and so I proposed at the PCC that we should have the new Series 2 service at that service only, and said I was not prepared to consider using it at the 8 a.m. Communion. A protest was immediately lodged – as I knew it would be: 'Why can't we have it at our service?' A motion was proposed that Series 2 be used at all Communion services, and when the vote was taken the vicar was triumphantly defeated.

But at Bushey Heath, Series 2 was already in use, and when the modern language Series 3 was published, the PCC demanded, without any cunning on the vicar's part, that we used it even before the General Synod had actually authorised it. This time I was genuinely defeated, because I did feel that on occasions we ought to use the Book of Common Prayer, but the PCC would have none of it.

Eventually, we did produce a traditional language service for use at mid-week Saints' Days Sung Eucharists, based on Rite B of the Alternative Service Book, with permitted Prayer Book alternatives – roughly the old Interim Rite and what most people mean when they say they want a Prayer Book service.

I came to see that I had made one serious mistake. Myles Raikes had found when he came to the parish that there were four services with four separate congregations. These he had tried to combine into one, in the end dropping the said Communion service at 8 a.m. on Sundays. I continued this practice for some fifteen years. When I restored it, people returned who had left not through any disagreement but simply because they were being deprived of the service through which their needs in worship were met – a quiet service, yes, but more to the point one in which the language Cranmer gave to Anglican worship was used.

It is an arrogance on the part of the Christians to imagine there is only one way to God in worship, and it is an arrogance that catholics, evangelicals, charismatics, supporters of the ASB and of the BCP all fall into from time to time. Certainly one parish cannot provide all forms of worship, and it is right that care should be taken that the chosen form is the best of its kind that can be offered to God. At Bushey Heath I always resisted pleas to introduce a non-eucharistic Family Service, partly because I believed that Christian worship should be centred on the Lord's own service – which is itself at best *the* family service – but also because I knew I could not do it well enough because my heart was not in it.

Bishop Trillo left to become Bishop of Chelmsford, and was replaced by Victor Whitsey, a remarkable and forthright Lancastrian who had been curate at St Laurence's Chorley just before I came to serve my title at St Peter's in that town. Bishop Runcie told his Bishop's Council that he had appointed Victor because 'now that I'm a bishop, no one tells me the things I don't want to hear, but he will do so.' Do so he did, and in no uncertain tones. Robert Runcie found he did not like it after all, Victor Whitsey was 'moved upstairs' to be Bishop of Chester, and Runcie never again appointed anyone with that particular quality.

After Victor's first Easter in the diocese, I happened to bump into him. 'Did you have a busy Holy Week?' I asked. 'No one wants to see a bishop in Holy Week,' he replied. I went home and wrote immediately to invite him to preach at Bushey Heath every evening of Holy Week the following year, 1972. When the time came, we made an effort to use it as an evangelistic occasion. We sent a personal invitation to everyone who worshipped regularly, irregularly and rarely, asking them to fill in a reply card. A small group on the PCC were convinced that there was also a vast army of well-wishers who were on the verge of church attendance and awaiting only an invitation from the vicar. I encouraged them (without much conviction) to produce names, and as a result I sent out eight hundred further invitations. Six people replied and two came to the services. But we did have two hundred folk in church every night during that Holy Week. Vic Whitsey preached for thirty-five, sometimes forty-five, minutes and held the congregation spellbound. It had a profound effect on church life as well as starting a Holy Week tradition which continued over the years.

Soon after I arrived in Bushey Heath, I was asked to establish house groups. There were eventually eight of them, each with ten to twelve members, meeting monthly. All were eucharistic – that is to say, they began or ended with an informal Communion service – so they became a considerable pastoral commitment for myself and my curate, James Grindell and his successor, Philip Buckler. But they had an immense effect on the spiritual life both of the parish and of many of the individual members.

We were a very mixed community: professional people, commuters, white- and blue-collar workers, a large RAF estate of fairly senior officers mainly attached to the Ministry of Defence in Whitehall, many retired people, including twenty-four retired Church Army sisters living in Church Army accommodation.

These remarkable old ladies were both a source of strength and at times a cause of fairly innocent hassle. All had had posts of responsibility and many wanted to organise each other in retirement. Once I went to visit two of them in the Cottage Hospital where I was chaplain. 'I know who you've come to visit,' said the ward sister, who was also the wife of the Methodist minister. Her eyes twinkled. 'You'll find them at opposite ends of the ward – I've had to separate them! Why are Christians always the most difficult patients?'

But it was good to have what amounted to a religious community in the parish, where daily prayers were said in the chapel. One who was there in my early days, Sister Stubbins, claimed to have converted the great evangelist, Tom Rees, and always when I visited her would clutch my arm like the Ancient Mariner and tell me, 'I pray every day that the Lord will convert you, Vicar.'

Sister Dibb was at the evacuation of Dunkirk and would relate how, desperately thirsty, she knocked at a door and asked for a glass of water, only to be refused. Sister Barton, devout but excessively difficult, told me how, having for a time survived both heart disease and cancer, she once actually died. She travelled though a dark tunnel to emerge in sunlight on a grassy bank. There the Lord came to her and told her she had to return: 'We aren't ready for you yet'. 'You could certainly see his point,' my wife commented.

Perhaps the most remarkable was Sister Letitia Whitworth. At the first meeting of the house group which she joined, we went round the room introducing ourselves. One member was a senior civil servant for the Inland Revenue, another travelled the world as a salesman, another was a senior policeman. Sister Whitworth was the last to speak.

'Now it's your turn,' said a member in a kind voice. 'I'm sure you must have had a very interesting life.' It was said in a tone which suggested that she had done nothing more exciting than serving tea at a church fête. 'I suppose I have,' she mused. 'When I'd finished training, the Church Army sent me out to China. We had to travel by boat for two weeks up the Yangtse river and on the way I was captured by pirates. They treated us quite well really and when they realised that there was no money for our ransom, they let us go.' Beat that if you can!

Bobbie often reminds me that when we first married I told her, 'I am not a committee man – I don't sit on any more than I have to and I won't ever do so.' Before I left Eaton Bray, I was on the newly established Pastoral Committee, the Diocesan Education Committee and secretary of its Laity Training Committee. To my surprise, in 1967, Bishop Gresford-Jones had asked me to be diocesan adviser in Clinical Pastoral Care, which kept me busily involved in lecturing and organising courses in Dr Frank Lake's clinical theology.

I had seen this new discipline as a means by which pastors gained insights into their own needs and personalities and also were enabled to identify possible psychological roots to pastoral problems presented to them, so that they would know when they could help and when they should encourage someone to seek medical or psychological help. By the time I left Eaton Bray, I had become uneasy at the number of clergy nationally who, far from being enable to recognise their own lack of expertise, had begun to see themselves as semi-skilled psychiatrists. This was dangerous and I had decided to withdraw gracefully.

When I moved, the decision was brought to a head. Synodical government had been introduced and I was horrified to find a new group established who seemed to me to be indulging in the worst kind of politicking. It was the New Synod Group, later to be named (or misnamed) the Open Synod Group. I decided, without much hope of success, to oppose the candidates they were putting forward and, with the support of my chuch-wardens, to put my name in the hat. At one point I was dropping behind, and under the system of the single transferable vote, was within a hair's-breadth of elimination. Then an Anglo-catholic candidate was eliminated and, though I had not stood as a cath-olic, almost all his votes were transferred to me. I leaped ahead, and ended as the third of the four successful candidates, beating all four New Synod Group members. A new experience opened up which deserves a chapter on its own.

For the parish, there were many benefits which more than outweighed my occasional absences. New ideas were discussed as soon as they came on the synodical scene; I was able to come to know and then invite distinguished preachers to Bushey Heath; and it brought a new dimension to my own preaching in the parish.

But I gradually became aware that it had a curious effect on my relationships with those who had elected me. In the deanery it was perhaps understandable. Whenever a new policy was sug-gested at the deanery synod, one of the Bushey Heath lay repre-sentatives would chirrup, 'Oh, but we've been doing that at Bushey Heath for many years'; or worse, 'We used to do that but we've moved on to something else.' I kept silence and mused on the pigeon-hole for the reactionary and out-of-date into which synodical liberals were wont to place me.

At diocesan meetings, it was rather more hurtful. I only needed to open my mouth at a meeting or diocesan synod to become the butt of ridicule or the practised sneer. I did not always (or often, to be truthful) take it in a Christian manner. Once I was cornered during a residential meeting of the diocesan synod. 'George, do you always make such a fool of yourself at the General Synod as you do here?' asked one member who was to become a suffragan bishop. His little group of friends sniggered. 'Funnily enough,' I replied, 'at the General Synod I'm listened to by people I respect, whereas in the diocese I'm patronised by people I don't respect.'

I expect I was rather obnoxious anyway, and remarks like that – quite apart from not being proper for a Christian – were hardly likely to win friends and influence people. But though I was vigorous in debate in putting forward my own point of view, I have never used the increasingly common technique of personal attack.

The most hurtful I suffered came from a member of the senior staff (that is to say, the Bishop's immediate staff). I had been asked at the Bishop's Council to liven up a debate in the diocesan synod so that the subject would be better aired. I had no strong views and cannot even recall the subject. But I agreed, reluctantly, and the debate produced many useful speeches. At the end, the senior staff member summed up, answering points which had been made. Almost at the end, he said, 'Now I come to George Austin's contribution. There are clergy who spend so much time at Synod that they neglect their parishes ...'

I was stunned and sickened. I sat white-faced at the gale of sycophantic laughter which burst forth, while the remainder of his comments went over my head. The debate then ended and we broke for lunch. Canon Geoffrey Edwards, one of the most senior priests of the diocese, was sitting in front of me and he turned round. 'That,' he said, 'was the most disgraceful thing I have ever heard a diocesan figure say of one of the clergy.' It was also defamatory – as well as totally unjustified – and I immediately went to demand an apology. He did later give a half-hearted one to the synod, but he could not see that he had done anything out of order: 'It's just the cut and thrust of debate, George!'

But not of debate in a Christian synod.

However obnoxious I may have been, I did find diocesan attitudes hard to take. Quite apart from serving as a diocesan member of the General Synod for nearly twenty years – twice easily topping the poll – I had been diocesan representative on the Central Board of Finance for the same period, and in the diocese itself at one time or another a member of the Bishop's Council, the Board of Finance, the Pastoral Committee, the Education Committee and many sub-committees. I had tried to serve the diocese and those who elected me conscientiously and faithfully, ready if necessary to put my head above the parapet, even when I knew it would damage any prospects of preferment which I might have had. Nevertheless events were to prove once again the truth of the lesson I had learned years before, that because one is paranoid, it does not necessarily mean one is not persecuted.

I was puzzled rather than angry when members of the senior staff seemed to take a delight in making life difficult for me. In the St Albans diocese, it was the custom for incumbents not to attend when the archdeacon made his visitation to the parish. It gave churchwardens – and I welcomed this – the opportunity to raise parish problems with the archdeacon, including problems with their vicar.

On two occasions, however, it worked the other way round. One archdeacon told my wardens that they were having problems with me. Unaware of this, they asked him in what way. 'Undertakers can never get hold of him. I haven't time now, but I want to come over again to discuss it with you,' he added. An appointment was made and in the meantime I asked the undertaker who dealt with most of our funerals, what was the problem. He was astonished: 'There isn't any problem. I can get hold of you more easily that I can any of the other clergy. And anyway, if there was a problem, I wouldn't raise it with the b—— archdeacon, I'd raise it with you!'

The churchwardens, however, had their own way of dealing with awkward archdeacons. When the day came, the archdeacon had barely begun his complaint about me when he was interrupted by one of the churchwardens, then a tough and forthright detective-inspector of Scotland Yard's Robbery Squad and himself the son of a priest. 'Look here, archdeacon, if you've got some vendetta going against our vicar, don't try to use us. We're not getting involved and if you've nothing more constructive to say you can b—— off.'

I am sure there must now be a red warning sign on the archdeacon's file on Bushey Heath. Unfortunately it was not there in those days, and another unwary archdeacon fell into the trap of taking on my churchwardens. There is always someone in a parish who believes God has called him – or more likely, and in this case certainly, her – to be a (deeply committed Christian of course) trouble-maker. Their tittle-tattle, usually exaggerated, highly coloured or just plain false, can cause much trouble and heartache. In this case it reached the archdeacon's receptive ears.

'I'm told your vicar is never seen in the High Road,' he pontificated ponderously to the churchwardens. Now it so happened that I actually lived on the High Road, and it was rarely that I was not up and down to the shops and the post-box two or three times a day. 'I don't know what it is you've got against our vicar,' one churchwarden responded, 'but I can tell you this. If I'm sick or if I have a problem, the vicar will be on my doorstep that day. And that's all I ask of my priest.'

Both in Bushey Heath and in Eaton Bray I was blessed with excellent, efficient and, above all, loyal churchwardens. And that loyalty included the ability not to see the vicar as always in the right – or, worse, always in the wrong – but to be ready to defend him when he is right and tell him when he is wrong.

After I had been at Bushey Heath for some fourteen years, I began to feel, reluctantly, for we were all very happy there, that it was time to move. I trusted the churchwardens sufficiently to be able to share this with them. I knew they would tell me the truth, not agreeing simply because they saw it as a golden opportunity to get rid of me nor disagreeing because they were happy as they were. Both of them, and the lay chairman of the PCC, confirmed my feeling that it would be good for me and for the parish to have a change.

But to what? Years before – in 1972 or 1973 – Bishop Runcie had called me to his study to tell me that I had been 'put on the list' of potential suffragan bishops and archdeacons. It was unexpected and I was quite flattered. But I did not take it as seriously as some who have been given the same glad tidings. And some bishops do seem to use the promise of future glory to curb the excesses of priests who might otherwise be a thorn in their flesh. Indeed not a few have had dramatic Damascus Road conversations on learning the news, abandoning unpopular views more easily than they would discard a worn-out pair of shoes.

In Bishop Runcie's case, it was more likely to have been an act of kindness and support to an insecure priest. Certainly, if it had been with any other motive, it was singularly unsuccessful. But it did also coincide with a long period in the church's life when the cult of mediocrity was in the ascendant. It was acceptable to rock the boat of traditional orthodoxy – even to open the stop-cocks. But to challenge the assumptions of a growingly powerful liberal élite was the ultimate *faux pas*, the sin against an interpretation of the Holy Spirit's guidance for which there was no forgiveness.

I spoke out vociferously for everything in doctrine, morality, holy Scripture and social affairs, that liberalism seemed ready to abandon, so it was hardly surprising that no more was heard of my presence on 'the list'. But I enjoyed being a parish priest, and anyway had never seen ministry and vocation in terms of a secular career structure. Short of the occasional pang when some gained preferment for no better reason than that they were ready to sell their integrity for a mess of episcopal pottage, I had not a single regret.

But when I began actively to seek a move from Bushey Heath, I found that every possibility seemed blocked. It was made clear to me that I would be considered for a senior canon residentiary's post with a strong in-service training responsibility and that

I was the dean's choice when the vacancy arose. Then the Downing Street appointments adviser stepped in and insisted that his office would appoint. When I was short-listed, I knew it was a formality that someone else would get the job. In the event, the person I had thought would be more suitable anyway was appointed.

Various posts swam into my ken and as quickly swam out, even in one case prompting Archbishop Runcie to say to me, 'I thought you were going to be made Archdeacon of X?' No one had asked me. I was invited to apply for the post of principal of a theological college, to which as a non-academic I thought I was unsuited. It had in any case a reputation for liberalism into which I hardly fitted. I discussed it with the Bishop of St Albans, who advised me only to apply if I was 'officially' invited to do so. I consulted the person (a diocesan bishop) who had approached me about it, and he came back to me with the information that I was to consider myself 'officially invited'. I applied and was not even short-listed – a lack of professionalism on the part of the college which assured me of a lucky escape.

My generation of clergy are not enthusiastic about the modern tendency to apply for posts, since we were brought up in the tradition that to apply was to invite immediate rejection. It simply was not done, and one awaited the 'call'. But after two years of frustration, I was left with no alternative.

I spoke to clergy I knew who were involved in university and college patronage – where appointment to a parish is, for historical reasons, in the gift of a particular Oxford or Cambridge college. I asked to be considered for vacant livings in my own diocese and as well I applied for vacancies in other dioceses. One of these was in a centre for theatre and the arts, and the people wished to have a greater involvement alongside the secular centres of the complex. The patrons were the dean and chapter of a cathedral where the dean was a fanatical supporter of the Movement for the Ordination of Women, so it was hardly surprising that, even with the bishop's support, I was not even considered. it was all very humiliating and probably good for me.

Then the Bishop of St Albans invited me to consider the parish of St Leonard's, Flamstead. It had a population of about 1,500, with a regular attendance not much less than Bushey Heath and about twelve per cent of the total population on the electoral roll of the church. There had been a long and faithful catholic tradition, and they were keen to have a priest who would continue this. But for some years it had been thought of as less than a full-time commitment, and the Bishop told me it would give me more chance to write and speak on the matters which concerned me. I met the churchwardens and parish representatives and we liked each other. I accepted the Bishop's offer, and looked forward to ending my ministry among these friendly and supportive folk, and to worshipping in their beautiful medieval church.

By now, I had become a 'media' figure – not by choice or inclination, but rather because I believed I had been given the opportunity to speak out against the trends current in the Church's life and felt I had a duty to make the most of them. As a result, the *Daily Mail* did a piece on the appointment, suggesting that a dissident and troublesome priest had been demoted. To the great amusement of the people in Flamstead, an editorial in the same issue suggested that this was the equivalent of being sent to Siberia and that it was sad that the Church treated its faithful priests in this way. It may have been over the top, but there was some truth in the general points it made.

I soon had a furious archdeacon on the phone, telling me I must ring the editor and demand a retraction. 'Oh,' I said innocently, 'do you mean you want me to tell him the whole truth?' For the whole truth was that we were leaving a parish where we had one of the best vicarages in the diocese for one where the departing vicar and his family had found clothes in wardrobes wet and mildewed, and curtains ruined by the black mould which flourished on the interior walls. Indeed, had it been a council flat, it could well have appeared on Esther Rantzen's *That's Life* as an example of the iniquities of council landlords. And because the parish was poorer than Bushey Heath, it could not pay the full expenses of the incumbent so I might have been £1,000 a year worse off financially. The archdeacon did not press the point, and I did not feed this juicy tit-bit of information to my journalist friends.

Then something happened which threw me into turmoil. I had attended a meeting of the Central Board of Finance, where I sat with the Bishop of Hull, Donald Snelgrove. For many years, we had whiled away dull moments at the CBF sharing the latest funny story. This time I told him I was on the move, to Flamstead. 'You can't do that,' he said. 'You should hang on and something better will come.' I explained that I was very happy to go there and that, anyway, it had been made clear to me by the diocese that it was this or nothing. He continued insisting, quite vociferously, that I was making a mistake, so much so that I began to smell a rat and suspect that there was something more to it. Two days later I knew why: a letter, hand-written and three pages long, arrived from the Archbishop of York, John Habgood, asking me if I could extricate myself from Flamstead and inviting me to become the Archdeacon of York. I was stunned.

But how could I go there? I had accepted Flamstead because it seemed what God wanted me to do for the rest of my life in the ministry. Jeremy was about to leave school and needed family around while he tried to get into his chosen career of journalism. Bobbie was happy in her job, by now deputy headmistress of a multi-racial school in Watford and much involved in plans for a new school which would open in a year's time. And her father was declining rapidly and might well have to come and live with us. No, York was impossible.

I asked one or two friends, in the strictest confidence, and each was adamantly insistent that I must accept. In his letter to me, John Habgood had said that although we had had some very public disagreements, we had always remained friends – but we had certainly disagreed. Only recently I had so criticised statements he had made at the time of the Garry Bennett *Crockford's* affair that I had suggested, in a television interview, that Dr Habgood was totally unsuitable to become Archbishop of Canterbury.

Yet here he was offering me a job like this. And if he can offer *me* such a job, I thought to myself, then he is the sort of man I should like to work for. I veered daily between acceptance and refusal. However, it so happened that Dr Habgood was going into hospital for a minor operation which would put him out of action for three weeks, and I was going as part of a study leave to spend three weeks in the United States. We had already arranged a holiday in the Yorkshire Dales at the May half-term holiday, so I asked if I might come over to York to talk about it all.

I awoke on the Sunday morning of the holiday and it was for the first time clear in my mind that I must accept. But for Bobbie it would, I knew, be a nightmare prospect and I waited to see if the Archbishop would be happy for her to continue working, commuting at weekends between York and Bushey. That was no problem, he told me: our domestic arrangements were our own concern and nothing to do with the job.

I met up with Bobbie, who had had a happy day walking round York with her father, having found the city not at all like her picture of the north of England. In the evening, I told her I had decided I ought to accept, and we went to bed unhappy, with Bobbie a little tearful.

But my wife is nothing if not a remarkable woman. I awoke the next morning to be greeted by a fairly content and highly practical Bobbie. Her father had already come to live with us, and so, with the proceeds of her family house as the deposit, we would take out a mortgage and buy a three-bedroomed house somewhere around Bushey or Watford. I could stay there when I came up to London (the Archbishop was keen that I should continue my London and Synod attachments) and Bobbie would drive up to York at weekends and school holidays. Wouldn't she mind the two-hundred-mile journey? I asked. She dismissed the problem: 'Oh, that's nothing – it's all motorway. And anyway, it will be like having a country cottage to get away to.'

And so it was. We had a very happy two years before she decided to resign from teaching, and, as an archdeacon with Saturdays now free from weddings, we probably saw more of each other than we had done for many years in the busy life of Bushey Heath.

When we were eventually able to announce the appointment, it proved a minor sensation. I had gently eased myself from the Flamstead post, and long afterwards, on a tentative visit to the church there while staying with the vicar, my long-time friend Dennis King, I found that in fact the good folk had understood.

The liberal church newspaper, the *Church Times*, had head-lined the story 'Dissident to Become Archdeacon of York', and one letter-writer gently asked how someone who believed all the articles of the Creeds and accepted all the foundation formularies of the Church of England could be described as a dissident. What *had* the Church come to? What indeed?

In the diocese of St Albans, reception of the news was mixed. The Bishop and his suffragan, Ken Pillar, appeared genuinely delighted, but one or two others of the senior staff seemed a mite concerned at the implications of the appointment. I had been an honorary canon of the cathedral since 1978, and heard that some-one at the cathedral, a convinced liberal, was putting out the 'news' that 'we know that John Habgood has stitched George Austin up firmly in order to silence him.' It was a curious piece of character assassination to imply that the Archbishop would behave in such a manner, but I have always found the thought processes of the less intelligent among the liberal establishment hard to fathom.

It was a great wrench to leave Bushey Heath, where we had spent eighteen happy years and where Jeremy had spent the whole of his childhood. He had had the two attic rooms as bedroom and sitting room and these had become the focal point for all his friends. Sometimes on a Saturday there were as many as twenty teenagers there and we would spend the whole evening answering the front door to let them in. I think it may have been hardest of all for him when the move took place.

For us it was not so much the house but all our friends who were hard to leave. In eighteen years, a parish priest shares many things with his parishioners – joys as well as sadnesses: births, weddings, the death of parents or sometimes of a child, growing disabilities and long sicknesses. All that is part of the job, and it builds relationships which can never be broken or replaced. We would especially look forward to Christmas and Easter when families were reunited. Children we had seen grow up, become engaged, and then marry and move away, would return for the festival, and it was always a joy to welcome them back. A parish priest is a member of a family much wider than his own, and it is the greatest of privileges.

I had intended to leave Bushey Heath for Flamstead at the beginning of September, and although my collation as archdeacon was not until November 19th, I decided I should stick to the September date. It would give a longer break before the new incumbent, and anyway, had I stayed on, it would have been a period of indecision and uncertainty for the congregation, who were already geared to my September departure.

The last weeks were both happy and sad. We were invited to dinner by family after family and it was good to know we had so many friends. The most touching moment for me was at the farewell after my final service.

No one who had been vicar of the same parish for eighteen years has escaped making mistakes. Many of them. I knew as I looked round the people in the congregation on those final Sundays that I had failed many of them when it mattered most. When a young son had died painfully of cancer, when a husband had left for a younger woman, when a much-loved cousin had been murdered, when – when – when ... There were too many 'whens' to recall.

Yet it was those very people whom I thought I had failed who came to me privately and thanked me for what I had done or said on those very occasions when I had felt the greatest sense of inadequacy. Of course, the truth is that I *had* been inadequate. But any priest knows that when Jesus told his disciples not to worry, that 'in that day' the Holy Spirit will give the right words to say, it was a promise not just to his disciples but a promise too to today's pastor.

Chapter nine

Party Games

Gallia est omnis divisa in partes tres   De Bello Gallico—Julius Cæsar

Like Gaul, the General Synod is divided into three parts; the Houses of Bishops, Clergy and Laity. But as well as being divided into three parties: the Catholic Group, the Evangelical Group and the Open Synod Group, called in the early days the New Synod Group. Legend, fostered by leader-writers of the *Church Times*, has it that the Catholic Group is peopled by black-suited priests and compliant laity who are whipped in a solid block into the voting lobby – usually that of the *Noes* – fodder for whatever reactionary whim is presently afflicting the group's Mafia godfathers.

As is often the case, fact fails to mirror fiction, and meetings of the Catholic Group are more often than not marked by a wide divergence of opinion on almost every issue. Rarely do members of the Group march in a single body through the same voting door.

Evangelicals are seldom pilloried in the same way, perhaps because in spite of a historical association with muscular Christianity they are less vigorous in debate and more circumspect in the expression of their opinions. Like catholics, they are united by a common tradition and practice, and the similar internal differences they experience arise not from any divergence of views in fundamental doctrine but rather from the varied ways in which members wish to see their practical expression.

Once separated from catholics in the Church of England by a distrust of ritual and a less sacramental approach to worship, evangelicals have in recent years found common ground in an appreciation of the centrality of the Eucharist, as catholics have learned the richness and power of the evangelical understanding of Jesus as personal Lord and Saviour.

As the faith itself has been increasingly threatened by the intrusion of liberal theology and secularism into the Church, the two groups have discovered that the fundamental truths which unite them are more solid and permanent than the peripherals which appear to divide them.

In the earliest days of the new Synod, there was in fact a fourth group: the Non-party Group, whose members did not wish to be identified with any of the three major groupings while nevertheless often sympathetic to the aspirations of one or other of them. I attended its first meeting after the 1970 election and found myself elected to be a joint secretary.

There are 550 members of the General Synod, and it is an advantage to belong to a smaller grouping in which one comes to know well a smaller number of people when it is quite impossible to know the whole membership. And there is value too in teasing out some of the issues to be debated before the main debate takes place on the floor of the Synod.

But even as early as that first group of sessions of the Synod in November 1970, pressure began to be exerted on members of the Non-Party Group to allow themselves to be absorbed by the New Synod Group. After all, was not this new group meant to be precisely that: a non-party group in which all shades of opinion might be represented, with no unhealthy pressures from party whips and a respect for the integrity of varieties of opinion?

Unfortunately for this point of view, members of Synod were there for the most part because they had just taken part in an election – an election in which no group had campaigned more vigorously than those who claimed New Synod allegiance, and who represented views which many members of the Non-Party Group were pledged to oppose. I was one of them, and later returned to my natural home in the Catholic Group.

Nevertheless, in those early days lasting friendships were made which crossed all the party divides. Indeed, the first ten or even fifteen years of the Synod's life were a pattern for the Church as a whole in the proper expression of Christian controversy. We argued vigorously but never personally, respected the integrity of those with whom we were in dispute, yet remained able to walk together as friends in the house of God.

Much of the blame for the fact that this is no longer so must, I believe, be laid at the door of the Open Synod Group. Many of its members genuinely see it as a body whose views transcend the Church's party divisions; but to its leadership (though not always to its chairman) it has been a vehicle for the promotion of the secular liberalism which regularly finds its way across the North Atlantic.

A senior member of Synod, who considered it his painful duty to attend meetings of all three party groups, contended that it was only in the Open Synod Group that he found any unanimity of opinion. In both the other groups, whatever the issue there was always some measure of a difference of opinion and always members who would be voting on opposite sides on contentious issues.

'No one's mind is more closed', said one bishop to me, 'than that of the open-minded liberal.' Certainly an intolerance of dissent has gradually infected the General Synod which is totally contrary to the comprehensive character of which the Church of England used to be so proud. Those who dissent from the Open Synod party line are always castigated as opposing the guidance of the Holy Spirit, being beset by a psychological fear of change, full of hang-ups, and needing the liberation which would come if only there was an uncritical acceptance of everything new under the sun.

Tension gradually built up as those who opposed the liberalism which seemed to be taking over the church felt more and more on the margins of that Church whose teaching they fully accepted. During the primacy of Robert Runcie a feeling grew that the marginalisation was part of a deliberate policy.

Some of us began to examine the pattern of episcopal appointments and, though we followed different criteria, we come to roughly the same conclusion: that catholics and evangelicals were being deliberately and systematically excluded from senior posts. It was noted that of the first twenty diocesan bishops appointed new from 1980 onwards (that is, who were not already diocesan bishops and translated to another diocese) no less than fifteen had a close connection with Dr Runcie – his two former suffragans, college and other close connections, and so on. And most came from an unquestionably liberal stable.

A member of the Crown Appointments Commission complained that a friend of mine, a priest on Synod, had asked her after one undistinguished appointment had been announced, 'Are you going to open a new barrel now? You've clearly scraped the bottom of the present one!' 'It's all very well,' she said, 'but you have to realise there are no catholics of sufficient calibre.' We were just going into a meeting of the Synod's Standing Committee, and when we broke for lunch I went across to her. 'In the light of what you said, I looked at the catholics present this morning,' I told her. 'I could see at least four who are each of higher calibre than the last half dozen you've appointed put together.'

One way or another, the concern was bound to become public. It eventually did so through the anonymous Preface to *Crockford's Clerical Directory*. There had been a long tradition that this annual preface contained a studied review of the Anglican Church, often with trenchant criticisms of policies and people. Bishops and archbishops had not escaped, and in the previous issue, harsher things were written of a bishop and a Member of Parliament than anything that appeared in 1987. But this time it was the liberal ascendancy in general, and Archbishop Runcie in particular, who were attacked.

I was interviewed on the day of publication by Brian Redhead on the BBC's *Today* programme. He asked me if I was surprised. 'No,' I replied. 'The surprise is not that the criticisms have been made but that they have not been made before now.'

It was significant that no one in the *Today* office had been able to obtain a copy of the Preface, even though the press had been provided with complete texts, and we had to rely on the fairly detailed extract in the *Times*. William Oddie explains why in his book, *The Crockford's File*: 'John Barton, broadcasting officer of the Church House Communications Committee was so incensed by the contents of the Preface that he refused ... to send it out.' This extraordinary act of censorship went unpunished.

I was one of those 'identified' by the media as author of the Preface, and not every journalist accepted my denial. But it was not my style. I never wrote anonymously; and it was too erudite and in too elegant prose for me to have been its author. I was a little put out by those who accepted the latter reason with rather too much enthusiasm.

Media pressure was certainly great on those suspected of authorship. My telephone hardly ceased ringing for nearly three weeks and I tried to give time to their questions – in fact building up the trust which I believe ought to exist between us.

For one person, the pressure was too great – Canon Gareth Bennett, ecclesiastical historian, member of Synod and its Standing Committee, fellow of New College, Oxford, and personal friend, confidant and sometime speech and sermon writer to Robert Runcie.

He had been pestered by the media certainly, but he had also been attacked as a disappointed cleric, as one bent on personal revenge, as the unknown author of a sour and vindictive piece which was unjustified in its assumptions. One senior religious journalist who had been totally convinced throughout that Bennett was not the author called me one day to say that 'official circles' (who? – I know not, save that it was certainly neither of the Archbishops nor anyone at Church House) were now saying, 'Don't ask us, ask Garry Bennett.'

Then one night, the telephone rang at about two o'clock in the morning. It was the *Times*. A voice said gently, 'I am afraid I have very bad news for you. Canon Bennett has been found dead in his car.' I shall always be grateful to my friend Clifford Longley, then religious affairs correspondent, for his thoughtful compassion at that time. He had asked a member of the news staff to let me know so that I would not read it first of all in the morning newspaper. So much for the callous lack of compassion often attributed to the media by senior churchmen. The deputy editor of the *Mail* – a paper much maligned at the time – told me that at one point he was so concerned for Garry that he had called off his team of reporters.

In truth, of course, we all felt guilt for the pressure under which Garry had been driven to take his life: the media, bishops who had criticised in so forthright a manner, friends who could not do enough because they did not know. My own guilt was that I had warned him of the report that 'official circles' had begun to implicate him. Any parish priest knows that guilt is a frequent part of bereavement. But that does not remove the guilt.

The Synod was stunned and for a time it seemed that maybe there would be a change of direction. Senior members of the Church of England began to ask themselves if there could be something deeply wrong when a distinguished scholar could feel so strongly as to write as he did and then be driven to suicide at the possibility of exposure.

There was a gloomy debate in Synod in February 1988 in which, instead of facing the issues raised by Dr Bennett, the Synod – with a pusillanimity which ought to have warned us that reluctant repentance would not lead to amendment of life – determined that there should no longer be an anonymous preface to *Crockford's*.

I made a plea in that debate for a return to comprehensiveness in our church:

> Above all else, we need, with all our differences, once again to recognise each other as members of the one church, with opinions to be respected and acknowledged for their integrity. We must have an end to the sneers, the abuse, the gratuitous

contempt which have become a malignant cancer eating away at the soul of our Church. We just cannot go on as we are.

It was – a little to my surprise – received with acclamation, and summing up the debate, the Bishop of Guildford accepted the criticism:

> What troubles many of us is when people give expression to this feeling of being strangers and aliens in this church of which we are all part. It is that feeling that we need to face, seriously and compassionately, and indeed make amends so that people in future do not feel it.

Alas, it was soon forgotten. The very next day in a debate on the Warnock Report, a speaker raised gales of laughter when she derided the deeply-held views of those who believe that human life begins at conception.

The preparations for the legislation to allow women to be ordained to the priesthood proceeded, and throughout the revision process and in Synod debates, all attempts to make it marginally more acceptable to opponents were resisted. Indeed, as the process moved on, amendments were allowed which merely added to the feeling that doors were being deliberately slammed in the faces of those who upheld the traditional view of the priesthood. Financial compensation was included for those who would feel they must resign, but the impression given was that this was a reluctant move to meet possible parliamentary objections. It is true that conscientious provisions were made, but few opponents have the slightest doubt that, as in other provinces of the Anglican Communion, these would be repealed at the earliest opportunity or just simply ignored.

Such views of course question the integrity of their proponents, some of whom are genuine in their concern to 'do the right thing'. That these views are held is a sad indication of the lack of trust which has developed over the years as the traditional and orthodox have come to feel increasingly marginalised by the dominant liberal establishment.

But after *Crockford's* there was certainly a perceptible change in the kind of bishop who was appointed. There were still definable liberals, though from a wider field; but there were evangelicals too, like Michael Turnbull, Pat Harris and George Carey, who did not rush to clamber on to every liberal bandwagon. Unexpectedly, one or two catholics opposed to the ordination of women – like Alan Chesters and Noel Jones – were appointed, and David Hope was translated to become Bishop of London. The Westcott/Cuddesdon/BBC cupboard from which so many had been found in the earlier 1980s now seemed firmly closed.

Even more surprising was the choice of George Carey as Archbishop of Canterbury after only a brief episcopate at Bath and Wells. In the run-up to his appointment, it became clear that neither liberals nor evangelicals would countenance the appointment of a catholic, even if there had been an outstanding candidate. Archbishop John Habgood of York was the obvious choice, from seniority, stature and intellect, but conservative liberal though he might be (on his own admission), his liberalism was highly suspect and unpopular in other circles. And Prime Minister Margaret Thatcher was herself surrounded by strong evangelical influences. The appointment of the evangelical Viscount Caldecote as chairman for this occasion of the Crown Appointments Commission seemed to clinch the matter, even with the nomination by the House of Bishops of John Austin Baker and Ronald Bowlby, both with impeccable liberal pedigrees, as their representatives on the Commission.

But which evangelical bishop would receive the prize? John Taylor of St Albans was tipped strongly, a conservative on many issues, a good teacher and preacher with long experience as a bishop, a kindly pastor yet with the reputation that he allowed extreme liberals to dominate his diocese. Then there was the gentle Michael Baughen of Chester, a former Vicar of All Souls'

Langham Place in London, where he gained the respect of catholic clergy in his deanery; or Keith Sutton of Lichfield, with an experience of the Anglican Communion gained on numerous occasions as Archbishop Runcie's representative. It is fair to say that no one mentioned George Carey, or if they did, the comment was always added: But he's only just gone to Bath and Wells.

Yet Carey it was. And it was a bold move, the significance of which only began to sink in slowly as the news was digested. I was asked to comment on the BBC's *Newsnight* that evening, and as we wandered round the Television Centre trying vainly to find the way out to the Blue Peter Garden where the interview was to be filmed, the interviewer commented that 'all the bishops we've spoken to seem delighted'. 'Yes,' I said, 'but did you notice the clenched teeth?' Would I say that on camera? No, I would not! For the appointment of George Carey at the age of fifty-four meant that a whole generation of bishops had been leapt over and left behind. Archbishop Runcie might reasonably have assumed that among the bishops appointed before the *Crockford's* affair were to be found not only his successor but also his successor-but-one.

Those of us brought up in the tradition that priesthood is for service, and that if preferment comes, it is to be accepted, but if not so be it, for there is no ladder to be climbed in the Church of God, find it hard to understand those whose ambition fuels them no less than people in secular employment. But it is so, and there are among the good and the great of the company of bishops a few whose ambitions are now thwarted. If they had any lingering doubts or faint hopes, then the translation of David Hope to London at the even younger age of fifty-one will surely have dissolved them for ever.

The 1990 elections to the General Synod were fought on one issue alone – the ordination of women. By now I was archdeacon of York and my seat was safe, a little 'rotten borough' with only three electors, the three archdeacons of the York Diocese. It is fair to admit that they agreed with me on only one issue: that the Archbishop had indicated he wished me to be the archdeacon on Synod for the York diocese.

But in the main the elections were heavily contested. In 1985 there had been the Durham factor, when the utterances of Bishop David Jenkins produced an adverse reaction against liberals. Would it be the same in 1990? Or would the expensive campaign financed and organised by the supporters of women priests swing the balance heavily in the opposite direction?

Women were particularly successful in the lay elections, but at least forty of them proved to be members of Women Against the Ordination of Women. For some, it was to be an eye-opener. One new member told me how she was enthusiastically welcomed by MOW (the Movement for the Ordination of Women) members who joined her for coffee, only to find she was dropped and frozen out just as quickly when they discovered she was not a supporter.

By 1990 there was little comparison with the new Synod of 1970, with its oppenness, friendly rivalry, and general acceptance that the Church of England was a broad, comprehensive church. It had not of course been an overnight transition.

I had been elected to the Standing Committee in 1985 for the first time, together with Garry Bennett and Canon Brian Brindley, and allocated to sub-committees. It is the practice that a small group of very senior and respected Standing Committee members, with a member from each of the three houses, presents suggestions for committees and other posts within the Standing Committee, and these are (or were) normally accepted.

Garry was put on the Policy Sub-committee and Brian and I to the Business Sub-committee, with Brian as chairman, a post which holds a special responsibility in the Synod rather like that of Leader of the House in the House of Commons. I enjoyed it, and the committee worked well together. Then came Garry's tragic death.

Canon Peter Dawes had at about the same time been

appointed Bishop of Derby, so there was a by-election for the two standing committee seats. They were won by Fr John Broadhurst and Dr John Sentamu, who then needed to be found sub-committee places. Garry Bennett's place on the powerful Policy Committee had to be filled by a member of the house of clergy who, to keep the balance, ought to be a catholic. John Broadhurst was too new and Brian Brindley well-established and highly efficient in his chairmanship. Which left me as the only and obvious choice.

To my surprise the Open Synod members challenged the recommendations – or rather, since there was nothing to be challenged in the other two appointments, objected – albeit obliquely – to my name. Lest any Standing Committee member should be in doubt, I offered to leave while the matter was discussed. It was not necessary, and the appointments were confirmed. We had won, but I knew it would not be forgotten.

Then, as a result of a foolish indiscretion, Canon Brindley was hounded out of the Synod. The redoubtable Dr Margaret Hewitt warned me somewhat dramatically, 'Watch out! Dr Bennett, Fr Brindley – you will be next on the list!' They would have a fight on their hands, I thought.

His departure meant a redistribution of posts within the synodical structure and once again the Group of Three suggested I ought to fill a particular office. I was enjoying the Policy Committee and anyway did not want the particular responsibility of the office proposed, not least because it meant a somewhat closer following of Synod debates than had become my custom. After twenty years, I had learned that almost everything of substance is said in the first half-dozen speeches, and after that, the place to be is not the debating chamber but the coffee lounge.

But I tend not to turn down jobs just because they are uncongenial, and I agreed that my name could go forward. It ought not to have been to my surprise that it was challenged, and referred back to the Three. They decided to return with my name and this time my anger was roused and I was determined that they should. I know that both Archbishops were asked if they approved, and that their agreement was obtained.

On the day of the Standing Committee meeting, I at once sensed that over the previous weekend, telephone wires had been hot and plans made to keep me out. As soon as the item was reached, the most political member of the Open Synod group objected and offered another name (who would be acceptable to evangelicals and who indeed I should otherwise have been entirely happy to see in the post). We left the room, and after some fifteen minutes, Archbishop Runcie emerged with the news that the vote had gone against me by one vote. As we broke for lunch, the Open Synod member approached me: 'You do realise that I had to do this.' 'Of course.' I found myself replying, 'and when you have to make personal attacks of this kind, I realise you have already lost your argument.'

I may well be accused of betraying Standing Committee confidences by relating this event, but I have carefully avoided naming other names or giving details of voting patterns of individuals. Secrecy, which is keeping from others that which they have a right to know, must always be distinguished from confidentiality, which is not revealing that which is the property of others to reveal.

I have told the story in as much detail because it marked an important step in my personal journey to faith. I have never found it easy to turn the other cheek when others do or speak evil against me, and I have always felt a cold physical pain in the pit of my stomach when I have felt it necessary to engage in controversy, knowing from bitter experience that those who disagree will match reasoned argument with personal scorn, and that friends who encouraged the action will not be there when the bullets start to fly.

My reply was nothing in itself, but the moment stays with me almost as a Damascus road. Suddenly, and in a moment, the pain and anger and frustration accumulated in years of controversy dissolved away, and even before I had finished speaking I knew that a weight had lifted from my soul and that I would not be hurt again. Jesus said, 'Blessed are you when men revile you and persecute you and utter all kinds of evil against you falsely on my account.' Now I *knew* it was true, and that it was true for me.

With the 1990 Synod, the position has hardened and it is not only I who am targeted. It is now clear that hard-line Open Synod liberals are determined at whatever cost to promote their own manifesto, and if it is necessary in the process to sweep all other views out of the way, then this will be done. It is a sad prospect for the Church of England at the beginning of a Decade of Evangelism, and it can only bring conflict and division.

But there was a further incident which marked a step forward in my journey which may prove even more crucial. As I looked at potentially divisive matters creeping forward towards the Synod's agenda, I had said to friends that I would not leave the Church of England on the matter of women priests, nor if scriptural standards of morality were set aside in Synod decisions, as I could avoid the one and ignore the other in that I could still preach scriptural truth whatever the Synod decided.

But the straw which would break my back would be the introduction of inclusive language for God. Already the official Prayer Book of the Anglican Church in New Zealand includes an alternative Lord's Prayer in which God is addressed as Mother, while in the United States vigorous attempts were being made either to depersonalise God to avoid terms such as Father and Son altogether or else to introduce fully feminist/goddess images. As each reverses the biblical revelation of God, I could only regard them as heretical. It is a basic and important Anglican understanding that 'what we pray is what we believe', and since I could not pray what I should officially be asked to believe, I should have to abandon my membership of the Church of England.

It seemed a distant, almost hypothetical, prospect until at an exposition of Scripture held during the January 1990 Synod, the speaker, Dr Tom Wright of Worcester College, Oxford, referred to the Holy Spirit as 'she'. While I was still fuming at this, I was asked by the religious correspondent of the *Telegraph* if the week was likely to produce anything controversial. I had told him that he had missed the most controversial item, when God the Holy Spirit had been addressed in this way. It is fair to add that Dr Wright took great exception when my comment was published in the next day's issue, insisting that he had used 'she' only of the Holy Spirit and not of God. But my understanding of the Christian doctrine of the Trinity is that 'the Father is God, the Son is God, and the Holy Spirit is God; and yet they are not three gods but one God.'

I raised this later at a meeting of the Policy Committee, together with another catholic member, and we had the customary lack of support from fellow-catholics. I expected to be attacked by the liberal members, but to my surprise, they too remained silent, and I was left to parry a sustained volley from some of the evangelicals present. At the end of a fairly good-natured discussion, I thanked those who had spoken for the courtesy of their response. 'But, your grace,' I said to Archbishop Carey, 'I feel I must now consider my position.' The Bishop of Lichfield passed me a note of sympathy assuring me of his prayers, and the Bishop of St Albans whispered his agreement with my position on the use of feminist language for God in public worship. I was grateful to them and felt less alone. Nevertheless, I was deeply shaken and wondered if I could continue to belong to a church which seemed to me to be capitulating with increasing rapidity to the secular influences sweeping across the Atlantic. The Gadarene swine had nothing to learn from the Church of England of 1990.

I passed the weekend in some anguish. How could I stay in a church whose leadership seemed ready to abandon the fundamentals revealed by God himself, when even some evangelicals defended what I had thought to be the extreme of liberalism, and catholics preferred to remain silent – for whatever reason – rather than put their heads above the parapet? Or was I wrong anyway, and arrogant to boot, to imagine I was the only one in step?

It was my wife who almost inadvertently brought me to the right conclusion. I do not see myself as a leader or spokesman or whatever, but Bobbie has insisted – and I now reluctantly have come to see that she is right – that people do look to me as one who has the position and opportunity to speak out on their behalf. She had begun to notice that the ordinary church-people whom we met in the many different churches where I preach Sunday by Sunday often sought me out to thank me for saying whatever I had said on radio or television or in the Synod. And moreover that this had happened similarly when we were in Canada, the United States and Australia. To leave the church would be to abandon them.

As I thought and prayed about it on the Sunday, the answer was suddenly there. Of course I must not leave – now or ever, regardless of whatever heresy the Synod (or the bishops) might embrace. The church is God's church and the gates of hell shall not prevail against it, and if so be that eventually only a small remnant holds on to its orthodoxy, God will one day raise up a new Keble or Pusey or Simeon who will restore the faith. And in the meantime that remnant must be fed, whatever the personal cost.

After all, when God calls any of us into his service, he never mentions anything about it being easy.

Chapter ten

Ecumenical with the Truth

I could not have imagined that my simple request for a holiday exchange, which began a friendship with Pastor Sven-Oscar Berglund of the Lutheran Church of Sweden, would eventually have taken me to travel on four continents.

In the early 1970s, there appeared in the church the beginnings of an encouragement towards in-service training for the clergy. I tried to spend a few days in each year in some kind of training or conference, often in a field which was new to me, in order to stimulate decaying parts of the brain. When I began to hear from Fr Sven-Oscar of difficulties the Lutherans were experiencing over the Leuenberg Agreement between Lutherans and the Reformed Churches, this seemed a suitably obscure area of study.

Eventually, I produced a paper which somehow found its way to the then Bishop of Leicester, Ronald Williams, who had been asked to suggest an Anglican name for a joint Anglican-Lutheran working party. He put forward mine, and I found myself for a cold December week in a Geneva nunnery, together with a Swedish professor who corrected my English, and an evangelical American Episcopalian, John Rodgers, who, as a venture of faith, was setting up a new seminary which now plays an invaluable role in preserving orthodoxy in that troubled church. And from Tanzania there was Martin Mbwana, later of the Anglican Consultative Council, and Bishop Kibira, whom I was later to meet on many occasions at the Lutheran World Federation Executive, at which I 'observed' for the ACC for a number of years.

This was a pleasant and none-too-onerous responsibility which not only took me to Holland, France, Switzerland, Germany and

Sweden, but even to Argentina and Brazil, vastly broadening my understanding of the world-wide Church of God. But through mixing with a tradition which hardly exists in England, I slowly gained a new concept of ecumenism.

My own paper to the Geneva working party had been on the nature of episcopacy, and I had suggested that Anglicans had much to learn from the Lutheran understanding of apostolic succession as the apostolic succession of the faith rather than in our terms as an historic succession through the bishops. And perhaps in our ecumenical approaches, Anglicans should be more concerned to recognise the exercise of *episcope* instead of the present concentration on the narrower catholic understanding of the three-fold ministry.

The paper was well received by the working party but went down like a lead balloon when reported to the ACC. Yet as the years progressed, I found a parallel concept emerging at the Lutheran World Federation Executive, that of unity in diversity. Efforts at unity between churches had consistently failed where schemes were put forward which sought uniformity of belief or practice, often with forms of words which plainly had one meaning for one of the participating churches and were interpreted quite differently by another. Somehow the dishonesty of ambiguity of this kind was overlooked in the sincere effort to break down centuries of Christian disunity. But now Lutheran theologians and ecumenists were beginning to ask whether, since the glory of God's creation is not in uniformity but in diversity, this ought not to be present in the church. Perhaps – and it seemed gross heresy to some! – the particular insights which one church brought to another were the very differences themselves. Maybe God intended these to be the jewels in the crown which is his church in the world.

I had by now become a member of the Assembly of the British Council of Churches, and tried to introduce these new thoughts into the discussions preceding the Covenant for Unity which occupied the minds of the member churches in the early 1980s.

134

Unfortunately, if the General Synod is now less open than it once was to the kind of debate which respects opponents, the BCC Assembly always had its own concept of democracy and dissent. Often it would have taken longer to read the wordy and pretentious motions than the amount of time which was allocated for debate. Amendments were discouraged (unless they made the original motion even more politically contentious for those who veered from the strict party-line), and anything which challenged the simplistic BCC view of the church and the world was manoeuvred or sanitised out of existence.

I do not sit easily under that kind of régime and I was wont to make a nuisance of myself. The worst kind of Militant left council had nothing to learn from the BCC in the technique of dealing with those who deviated from the politically correct norm.

A gentle and godly representative of the Free Church Federal Council once took me aside to say that he almost always agreed with what I said and thanked me for saying it. 'But why then don't you speak out in the debates and support me?' I asked him. 'Because I could not bear to have done to me what they have done to you,' was his chilling reply.

Even as distinguished a churchman as the late Dr Ernest Payne, an honorary president of the BCC, did not escape when he deviated. A former senior member of staff had resigned/been dismissed – one was unsure which – and had afterwards carried out a campaign in the press and elsewhere against some of the activities of the BCC, and Ernest Payne had begun to show some sympathy for his arguments. At once a senior ecumenist began to drop hints that 'of course we know Ernest is becoming senile – it's so terribly sad.'

The most virulent and unpleasant attacks on me came when I challenged the uncritical support the BCC was giving to the World Council of Churches Programme to Combat Racism. Though the BCC (and later the WCC) would dismiss me as a racist, I had in fact a record in that field of which I had no reason to be ashamed.

As a curate, I had stood out in Notting Dale against the racism I found rampant in the riots and their aftermath in 1958 and onwards, and I had been threatened in letters and on the phone and spat at in the street for my pains. And by the time that I had become a member of the BCC Assembly, I was vicar of a parish with a large Jewish population, and my wife was to be deputy head of a multi-ethnic school in West Watford.

So we experienced race issues from the sharp end, and I was well aware that when the local Jewish Synagogue, in common with others in north London, found it necessary to employ a security guard whenever the building was used for worship, there would be silence from a BCC which, had the same been true of a Black Pentecostal Church, would have organised protest marches and anti-Government pamphlets.

But the WCC Programme to Combat Racism, right though it was in intent, seemed to me to miss the point when it supported organisations which engaged in terrorist acts. Apartheid in South Africa and the white régime of Ian Smith in what was then Southern Rhodesia were quite clearly rooted in concepts which were basically unChristian, and it was right to challenge them. Moreover it was defensible to give humanitarian aid to groups in those countries which were suffering for their opposition to the evils of racism.

However, it seemed to me to be incontrovertible that if those organisations deliberately used tactics which a Christian could not support, then to give uncritical aid (and anyway who could say humanitarian aid did not end in the same financial pot as the money for arms and explosives?) was to condone that which was evil as well as that which was good. A guerilla war might be supportable, and much was made of the moral and financial support given to the French resistance during the Second World War. However, the *maquis* did not put bombs in stores and on buses which were intended to kill civilians, women and children as well as men. The most BCC leaders (and Synod leaders too, it must be said) would do was

136

to regret that innocent lives were lost in this way, and then to go on to support the aims of the 'freedom fighters' – a term which of course disinfects the more critical and accurate description, 'terrorists'. It would at least have been more acceptable for a Christian organisation to have expressed support for the aims but then to have added, 'but, however laudable the aims, we cannot condone the butchering of innocent men, women and children by acts of terrorism.'

There was an even more unsavoury aspect to the whole sorry episode. For the support was selective and selectively critical: Marxist and other left-wing organisations could expect more aid and less criticism than the more politically moderate, a preference which was continued even after a battle had been won. In Ian Smith's Rhodesia, the Selous Scouts gained an unenviable reputation for cruelty and mayhem and were deservedly condemned by the BCC and WCC. But after independence, when Zimbabwe's North Korean-trained Fifth Brigade behaved in much the same manner, the criticism was so muted as to be unnoticeable.

In 1975, I accepted a South African Government invitation to visit South Africa on a 'fact-finding' tour. Maybe that was unwise, and certainly it was used afterwards to the disadvantage of my position. But I had insisted that I should be allowed to meet opponents of the régime, and be entirely free to express my opinions during and after the visit.

This was honoured: I met politicians of all parties and colours (of whom I found the white deeply unimpressive); churchmen of many denominations, including unexpectedly radical Dutch Reformed clergy; dissidents under banning orders. And in spending an hour with the Minister for Justice – a notorious man whose department was responsible for much alleged cruelty – I was able to challenge the use of torture and other brutalities. Of course it was little enough, and it would be naive to imagine that its effect was other than totally negligible: but at least it was more than any who lectured me at the BCC had ever achieved.

If it had been intended by the South Africans to convert me, it had quite the reverse effect. Apartheid in practice horrified me much more than anything I could have learned from second-hand accounts; though at the same time I came back convinced by the spirit of the black Africans – not so much the leaders as the ordinary men and women whom I had been able to meet in hotels, hospitals and so on – that apartheid could not survive and moreover that they were in no doubt of that.

I was nervous before I went, and took the precaution of leaving (with a discreet and senior policeman I knew) a list of four or five names to be investigated if I happened to get into any dificulty. It was certainly the case that someone had had telephone contact with activist in South Africa, blackening my name and warning against any contact. A white anti-apartheid leader reacted angrily to their interference and took it quite personally: 'Who do they think we are?' he asked. 'Don't they realise we run risks to life and liberty every day by speaking out? Why should we be silent with you?' One senior black churchman subjected me to a thirty-minute racist diatribe – 'I have been advised about you' – which led me to write in the diary I kept of the visit: 'What has the system done to this good Christian man that he can express such hatred of me for the colour of my skin?' It was itself a sufficient condemnation of the evil of apartheid.

When I returned to England I continued to speak against the WCC grants, though now – not quite as the South African government had intended – with a personal experience of the evils against which the guerillas were fighting. More senior churchmen than I then was would contact me before a major debate, whether in the BCC Assembly or at the General Synod, encouraging me to speak out and assuring me of their support. It was the first time I became aware that when you challenge the establishment, brother, you are on your own!

All this did not deter me from pressing the point on every possible occasion, even though from time to time hints were dropped that it was doing my career prospects no good at all. That too was no deterrent to one who did not believe anyway that there should be career prospects in the Church of God.

Perhaps the most depressing debate was in July 1986, when the General Synod considered a report on South Africa from the Board for Social Responsibility. It took place against a background of violence in South Africa, perpetrated by the security forces on the one hand and radical elements of African National Congress on the other. In full view of international television teams, police action in the townships was brutal, deliberate and indiscriminate. One could only assume that where the press were not present, the repression was even worse.

But ANC violence was no less brutal, and beatings and executions were increasing, some by the terrible method of 'neck-lacing', while bombs were placed in stores and at bus stops, causing death and injury to victims of all races.

I proposed an amendment deploring the 'indiscriminate use of terror and violence against innocent men, women and children, whether perpetrated by the African National Congress or the South African government'. Archbishop Desmond Tutu had made a similar plea in South Africa, and it seemed a modest but appropriate comment to make in the circumstances. It did not deny the ANC members' right to defend themselves; nor did it suggest that the government forces had no duty to contain violence when attacked.

The official response came in what was perhaps the most chilling speech I ever heard on the subject. Of course we all deplored the violence and terrorist acts (not by any means a self-evident assumption!) but the Synod should not accept the 'lofty even-handedness' of the amendment. The ANC had tried the path of non-violence (which I had neither demanded nor even mentioned) but had been gradually driven to behave as they did by the violence they had suffered at the hands of the white government.

The Synod accepted this defence and so condoned the terror inflicted by those who executed their enemies by burning a

139

petrol-filled tyre around the victim's neck, or killed and maimed the innocent with their bombs in public places. I was sickened by it all and wondered what kind of church it was that I was serving.

It was a similar story in Namibia, where rightly the WCC, BCC and Synod had condemned the activities of the government security forces. But when stories of torture and killings began (as long ago as 1978) to filter through from SWAPO's own detention centres outside Namibia, they were at first dismissed as South African progaganda lies. Eventually, when both refugees and former detainees began to return, the full horror of the conditions in which they had been imprisoned was revealed. Far from being hostile propaganda, it was the truth. And the ecumenical organisations, with their commitment to helping the oppressed and powerless of the world, uttered not a word of criticism. Indeed, before I went to the WCC Assembly in Canberra, I was taken aside to be told, 'We hope no one will raise the matter of SWAPO detainees ...' (Someone else took me aside to express the hope that no one would 'ask questions about the WCC's refusal to condemn the Ceaucescu régime.')

I confess that when I was elected as a delegate to the 1983 WCC Assembly in Vancouver, I expected to be at an organisation totally dominated by Marxism. I have to say that it was not so, and I returned impressed and encouraged. The churches of Eastern Europe and the Soviet Union brought not politics but spirituality to the proceedings of the Assembly, without which its activities would have been much impoverished.

Although much of the WCC's social teaching was dominated by a hard-line and intolerant liberalism emanating from North America, the Faith and Order department was strong and its contributions both orthodox and impressive. Unfortunately, between 1983 and the 1991 Canberra Assembly, the forces of liberalism and extremism seemed to gain almost total dominance. The structures, together with the fact that some eighty per cent of delegates are new each time to the Assembly, give golden opportunities to those who would use the occasion to promote

140

whatever extreme is currently fashionable, and there is little doubt that the World Council is now almost entirely in the hands of the liberal and the theologically unorthodox. Unless it can reform itself – and quickly – it may well lose the support of major denominations. It would be a sad end to a once-fine organisation; and it would be a sad day for the church in the world. A human institution will always be far from perfect, but we need a world council of churches even if the WCC itself is apparently bent on self-destruction.

In my own journey to faith, it helped to nourish the new understandings of ecumenism which had had their birth in my experiences with the Lutheran churches. But more important, it opened my eyes to the secular influences which were beginning to sweep across the Atlantic and whose gestation in the thinking of groups within the Church of England was already becoming evident and dangerous.

Chapter eleven

Eightieth Archdeacon

I was collated as Archdeacon of York in a splendid ceremony in York Minister on Saturday 19th November 1988. I was first of all licensed in the Lady Chapel as a canon and as prebend of Riccall and then taken in solemn procession to the Chapter House where I was presented to the assembled canons, who sat in their niches like Time Lords from a *Dr Who* adventure. Having been divested of my robes, I was then led out and told to wait until summoned. After a few moments, I was called to return and put my robes back on again. I swore on oath that I would not reveal the secrets of the Chapter – the nature of which I have yet to discover – and was presented with a small loaf of bread.

Only family and close friends had so far been allowed to attend, but Evensong followed in the nave before a large congregation, including folk from Bushey Heath who had made the long journey north. The Cathedral organist, Philip Moore, had asked me to suggest an anthem which the choir might sing, and I was delighted that they chose the opening chorus of Bach's *Lobt den Herrn* – and as an exciting surprise, with a small orchestral accompaniment.

I knelt before the Archbishop to receive my cure of souls and was moved by its solemnity and conscious of the history. I was the eightieth Archdeacon of York in a line stretching back at least to the year 1093. The only other archdeacon to hold the prebendal stall of Riccall was one Thomas Hayter who became Bishop of London in 1761, but died of dropsy after just two months in office. Hayter owed more than his archdeaconry to his archbishop, for when his patron died he had left him the whole of his large fortune.

Another had a less happy relationship with the archbishop. William Fitzherbert's election to the see of York had been opposed, successfully for a time, by archdeacon Osbert, and when he died in 1154 in suspicious circumstances, Osbert was accused of serving him a poisoned chalice during Mass. The truth was never finally proved, and the archbishop was canonised as St William of York.

After my installation, Archbishop Habgood welcomed our guests and friends at a reception in St William's College, a medieval hall to the north of the minister. I reminded him that I had promised solemnly and at least three times that I would give my obedience to the Archbishop and his successors.

Thus began, unexpectedly, the happiest time of my entire ministry. I had enjoyed the life of a parish priest, and had looked forward to spending the remainder of my time before retirement with the people of St Leonard's Flamstead. I had thought the job of an archdeacon to be formal and fusty, concerned at best with vicarage drains and gutters, and at worst as a pain in the neck to the parochial clergy.

I had imagined fondly that there must be some kind of induction course for new archdeacons but it was not the case; and every archdeacon I spoke to gave me a different – and sometimes contradictory – picture of what the post entailed.

Who, I thought to myself, was the best archdeacon I had known? Without a doubt it was Basil Snell, Archdeacon of St Albans in my early days in the diocese. The BBC Television series *All Gas and Gaiters* was popular at the time, and in fact it was partly filmed in St Albans – and Basil greatly resembled the archdeacon of the series, played by Robertson Hare.

But Basil Snell, though he was efficient and knowledgeable about archidiaconal business, was also a great support to the clergy, and saw his role as one who enabled the clergy to get on with the job to the best of their ability with the minimum of interference. To make sure the vicarage drains and gutters were clear was to care for the well-being of the vicarage family; to be concerned for the contents of the church building was an opportunity for pastoral contact with an incumbent and his churchwardens; to look at parish boundaries was a way of easing clerical burdens and an opening to exploring their problems.

I soon discovered that Archbishop Habgood had launched me into the best job in the Church of England, and sometimes, as I drive round the lovely villages and country lanes of the Vale of York, the rolling hills of the Wolds and the majestic scenery of the North Yorkshire Moors, I have to pinch myself and ask, 'Am I really being *paid* to do this?'

I was to work particularly closely with the Bishop of Selby, whose area was contiguous with my own, and for the first two years, this was Clifford Barker. Clifford had served for the whole of the ministry in York and his experience was invaluable to me as a newcomer – and we hit it off from the moment we met.

I quickly found that John Habgood was very different from the popular image of the solemn, remote and reserved cleric – warm, friendly, and above all with a sense of humour which bubbled up throughout the monthly staff meetings. Like Christopher Mackonochie of my Dunstable days, he was an excellent boss, ready to delegate responsibility, firm in his decisions and supportive to his staff. When problems arose, there would be full and open discussion, and in the end he would ponder for a moment and then say gently, 'It seems to me, what we have to do is ...' One member of the senior staff muttered to me on such an occasion: 'The annoying thing is that he's always right!'

Apart from staff meetings, I saw little more of him than before. He had asked that I be the archdeacon on the General Synod for the York diocese, and so we continued to meet in London for the Standing Committee. On the first occasion that the Synod met, I spoke in a debate taking the contrary view to that which Dr Habgood had expressed, and apologised to him afterwards. 'Not at all,' he replied. 'That's why I've appointed you.' Well, when we discussed my appointment, I had said to him, 'You know, I can't change.' 'I don't expect you to,' was his firm reply.

He must surely have realised too that in appointing me, he was giving me at once a higher profile in some of the public utterances I would make. The Archdeacon of Canterbury has a special role in the Province of Canterbury, particularly in that he must attend every bishop's enthronement. York does not, and though some say he is the senior archdeacon of the York Province, I have found no evidence of this.

But 'Archdeacon of York' does have a ring to it and it at least sounds more important than, say, Archdeacon of Crewe. I soon became aware that journalists saw it like this and I began to find that half the messages left on my answering machine were from the media. I must be more cautious, I thought, while at the same time not wasting the opportunities in which my vocation seemed to have placed me. At the same time, I became more and more aware that every time I attended the General Synod or its Standing or Policy Committee, yet another divisive issue was emerging from what I came to identify as the liberal agenda.

During a sabbatical leave in the spring of 1988 (just after John Habgood had offered me the post in fact), I spent three weeks touring North America, meeting groups of clergy and lay people from the Episcopal Church and the Anglican Church of Canada. It was not a speaking tour, though I did preach a couple of times, but an occasion for me to listen to the many differing viewpoints dividing those troubled provinces.

It became clear that beyond the high-profile issue of the ordination of women there was another, as yet half-hidden, agenda of secular causes, much more divisive and infinitely more damaging than women priests – in particular the recognition of homosexuality as an acceptable Christian lifestyle, with the possibility of single sex 'marriage', the use of feminist or depersonalised language for God in liturgy, and the continued onslaught of an intolerant liberal approach to the doctrines of the Church.

I had thought these were far from encroaching on the life of the Church in England, which would naturally be more sensible and moderate than our wayward daughter across the Atlantic. I began to be aware that I was wrong – indeed that we had our own heresies to add to them. Although it seemed increasingly likely that the legislation on women priests would not reach the necessary two-thirds majority when the Synod eventually took is final vote towards the end of 1992, this would make little difference to the emerging agenda.

A forecast of business likely to come before the General Synod during 1991–95 was brought to the Standing Committee. It listed at least seven items which were likely to cause further division in the Church – and that as a Decade of Evangelism was being trumpeted as a cause for prayer and rejoicing. I decided to go public on my concerns.

The canons of York Minister are by statute entitled to preach once a year in the minister, and it so happened that in 1991 I had been invited on Sunday 8th September, an ideal date with everything coming to life again after the summer holidays.

I am sometimes accused of using the media, but in fact I had little idea of how to set about making sure that what I wanted to say was heard. I made enquiries and found that I must send a 'flyer' listing the main points of my sermon to the press and broadcasting authorities, with an offer to provide the complete text on request. I commented that it is only when one imagines one is not being controversial that the media heavens open, and that probably no one would take any notice anyway. 'You must be joking!' said my contact. 'If *you* say what I think you are going to say, it will certainly be taken up.'

I began to get cold feet, and wondered if I should drop the idea and preach an innocuous sermon on, say, the structure of the Book of Isaiah. But what of all the folk who wrote or spoke to me with roughly the same question: 'Whatever is happening to the poor old Church of England?' Did not someone really have to speak up for them? I decided I had to go ahead, regardless of the unpleasantness which would undoubtedly come my way.

I sent off my flyer, and faxed a copy of the sermon to the Archbishops of Canterbury and York, knowing that they would certainly be asked to comment. My nervousness as I waited to process to the minster pulpit on the Sunday morning was not eased when I saw the Archbishop's wife and daughter slip into their seats.

The minster does not attract large congregations and the great nave was about half full. Any experienced preacher can quickly sense whether or not his congregation is behind him, but I was aware anyway that many of the regular worshippers attended because they knew the sermon would be centred on a liberal attitude which was anathema to me.

I studiously avoided the subject of women priests, since I was talking of a harsher agenda, which some of those who supported women's ordination would find as distasteful as I do myself – and anyway, by then most people had made their decisions about that issue. Instead I spoke of the threats to orthodox doctrines of the faith, of the syncretism inherent in inter-faith worship, of the possibility of scriptural moral standards being eroded and rejected, and of the likely introduction of feminist liturgies. To avoid the disintegration of the Church of England, I suggested that the day might come when parish churches would have to declare their orthodoxy, and in effect provide havens for those who would otherwise be totally alienated. There would be a 'church within a church'.

The telephone began to be busy on the Sunday, the calls becoming incessant on the Monday. I already had a full diary and Bobbie was left to field all enquiries, for me to deal with when I returned home. Many were from the media, but to our complete surprise, there were well over a hundred calls from members of the public, simply saying, 'Thank God someone in authority in the Church has spoken for us!'

One message was from Dr Habgood asking me to call in and see him, and I wondered for a moment if I ought to put an exercise book down my trousers. I confess that it brought back feelings I had not had since I was sent to Miss Law for chalking on the cardigan of the girl sitting in front of me at the Infants' School.

The morning press had reported his comment that my sermon had reminded him of the Fat Boy in *Pickwick Papers* who had crept up to an old lady and said, 'I want to make your flesh creep.' He explained that it was a quote which immediately came to mind but that he then realised he could hardly use it on me – I am, shall we say, a little over-weight and he always makes a joke of refusing to serve me a second helping at staff lunches. At first he refused to identify it, until the *Daily Telegraph* reporter insisted that if he did not, the editor would make him read the whole of Dickens if necessary until he found it.

I had been highly amused rather than offended, and we went on to discuss the sermon in detail. He was of course aware of my concerns but simply could not agree that the scenario I had painted was at all valid, nor that the widespread concern within the Church really existed. We had a frank discussion and parted amicably, and with friendship unimpaired.

But the 'Fat Boy' comment has been unwise, and when the Archbishop of Canterbury compared me to Humpty Dumpty (quite innocently and without any thought of my size!) the effect of what the general public assumed to be a double insult was to swing public sympathy towards me. I had not been perturbed by the descriptions, and found that which followed in each case more offensive. I had quite deliberately set on one side the issue of women in the priesthood in my sermon, so to suggest that the purpose of my sermon was to frighten anyone – old ladies or otherwise – was an attack on my integrity. So in the same way was Dr Carey's charge that I was making words mean what I wanted them to mean.

Moreover, attacks of this kind from the two Archbishops encouraged other senior figures in the Church to launch into the now-expected personal abuse. The Dean of Winchester called for me to resign, the chief secretary of the Church Army wrote an article which accused me of saying precisely the opposite of what I had actually said, while others claimed I was using the pulpit to make a political point.

This spurred on the lesser clergy to join the attack, and the editor of the *Church Times* was bombarded with letters from people who had either not read the sermon at all or else had failed to grasp what I was actually saying. One clergyman with a score to settle almost burst a blood-vessel in his frenzy to write increasingly foolish letters to the press through which he seemed to feel he was kicking me when I was down.

But I was neither down nor out. For with every post came support from church people of all ages – six hundred letters when I stopped counting, and still dribbling in months after the event. About three per cent were critical – mainly from clergy, who appear to have a gift for abuse unmatched by the laity. The worst, as always, came on re-cycled paper – I am unclear as to why environmentally conscious clerics have so developed an ability to write with such venom to fellow-Christians.

I found many of the letters deeply moving. Here were faithful members of the Church of England either still hanging on grimly by their fingertips or, more often and sadly, now totally alienated from the church they had served and supported perhaps for a lifetime. And not only Anglicans: not a few were from members of the Roman Catholic Church who said wryly, 'So you think you have problems ...!'

For every one who troubled to write, how many did that represent who thought of writing, or who would have written but did not know where to write, or who agreed but never wrote letters to people they did not know? Ten? or twenty? or a hundred? or more? Little wonder the church is losing members at a worrying rate.

The clerical insensitivity and arrogance hinted at in the letters was alarming. Many told of unfamiliar worship thrust upon congregations, and of promises to respect the worship needs of more traditional Anglicans broken and betrayed. And it was not so much a divide between those who 'like the Book of Common Prayer' or who 'can't stand the ASB'. These were often people who recognised that worship must change, that new methods must be used, that we must somehow reach the unchurched with the message of the gospel. But they themselves were being unchurched by arrogant clergy who dismissed that which brought them to God as irrelevant or even sometimes as unChristian.

Others too were alienated by the lifestyles of clergy who had taken to heart the permissiveness of the sixties and adapted their own patterns to conform to it. If in the minds of Christians there is an expectation that clerical behaviour must be exemplary – as Chaucer said, 'If gold rusts, what shall iron do?' – it is not that there is a double standard, one for clergy and another for the laity. Rather it is the same high scriptural standard, to break which seems to them so inconsistent with continuation in the priestly office.

A journalist asked me what was my next step, having been accused by other church leaders of setting a false scenario. I replied that I would simply wait until all that I had prophesied began to take place. I did not have long to wait.

On the day that the Archbishop of Canterbury's letter criticising my stand appeared in the *Times*, I was travelling up to London for a meeting of the Policy Committee. Dr Carey accused me obliquely of acting irresponsibly, and less obliquely of painting a picture which was totally false.

I put the newspaper down and turned to my papers for the meeting. In an overview of the next five years, I read that 'divisive issues coming before the Synod will include homosexuality and inclusive language'. Yet the Archbishop had asked, 'What are the grounds of his prediction that within five years our liturgies will be addressing God as 'she'?' My timing may have been wrong, but I did find it hard to square Dr Carey's rejection with the clear evidence of a Synod paper which he himself must have read. It would have made good copy for the press, but of course I was prevented from using this piece of evidence in my defence by the confidential nature of the Policy Committee document.

Further proof to support my case appeared before the end of the month, when a book of feminist services and prayers, *Women*

Included, was published. Already the official prayer book of the Anglican Church in New Zealand included an alternative Lord's Prayer in which God was described as 'Mother', and a similar (though, to be honest, rather better and much less clumsy) version appeared in this new unofficial publication. Contrary to Scripture though that was, there was much in *Women Included* which was even more offensive to orthodox Christians. I had in fact mentioned nothing about the influence of New Age religion in my sermon, but this intruded again and again into the text. The Jewish revelation of a God who is outside creation was rejected, with many prayers addressed to a god 'whose body is all creation' – like the Babylonian theophany in which creation is made from the gods themselves.

In a radio discussion on BBC Leeds, a woman deacon defended the new prayer book – which she claimed was nothing new and had been used in many Anglican churches – and insisted that there was nothing in it which was not Christian. I simply pointed her to the preface, written by an American woman priest who said quite categorically that 'this is the doctrine of panentheism, i.e., God is in everything and everything is in God.' She commended 'prayers to the earth' and spoke of 'these sources of feminine creation, contained in goddess and Celtic spiritual traditions, (which) help to satisfy our quest for new images.' Freedom of religion is a precious concept and I would not wish to inhibit anyone from making such a quest wherever they chose. But why do they have to subvert the faithful from the revelation of God in Holy Scripture?

There was more: for *Women Included* also undermined the doctrine of the incarnation, speaking of Jesus as one 'in whom Christians believe that God was especially present' – very far from the concept that Jesus is the Divine Word who was in the beginning with God and who is the Word made Flesh.

I had referred in my sermon to inter-faith worship and had declined to be one of the initial signatories of the proposed Open Letter because I did not wish to divert from the wider message I was attempting to present. But I did join the 2,000 clergy who

152

signed – and again that must represent many more who were in sympathy but who for one reason or another were not prepared to go public on it.

Once more, there was a bitter attack from the establishment, from those who quite reasonably questioned whether or not this would damage growing relationships with other faiths, to the downright silly who suggested that those who signed were racists!

The Osborne Report on human sexuality had been leaked on publication, though it was primarily an advisory report to the House of Bishops, who used it in the preparation of their own much more conservative document, published in December 1991. Though this was sadly hesitant to use the word 'sin', its style made much less likely the early fulfilment of my prophecy that the Synod would soon recognise homosexual genital acts as an acceptable Christian lifestyle or provide for the blessing of single-sex 'marriage'.

But 'less likely' is the operative phrase. In the end it is not what the bishops recommend but what the Synod decides which is the final arbiter, and there is little doubt that within the Synod there exists a strong body of opinion which supports the gay and lesbian lobby. In a *Sunday Times* poll of 200 Synod members following my sermon, nearly half believed that homosexuals should be allowed to make their own choices about their behaviour. Given the synodical tendency to let the heart rule the head, that is quite a sufficient number for waverers to bring them up to a clear majority.

I preached my sermon at the beginning of September in 1991, claiming that there was a 'liberal agenda' waiting in the wings of the Church of England. I was derided and ridiculed by leading members of the establishment. Yet by the end of that year, three of the four issues I raised and which, it was implied, were a figment of my imagination, had appeared at least on the fringe of our agenda.

It is true that this leaves them far from fulfilling the timetable I set out, and time will tell whether or not I am right. But the timescale was not my major concern. As I said in my sermon:

There is certain to be division in the Church, and we can now do nothing to prevent this happening. And in the process, much time and energy will have been expended which would better have been employed in spreading the gospel to an unbelieving world in a period designated as a Decade of Evangelism.

I do not want to spend those ten years in fruitless, barren disputes with those in the Church who disagree with me, even though I am bound to defend what I know to be God's truth.

That was the heart of my sermon and of my complaint. It is a desperately sad commentary on the present state of the Church of England that those leaders who attacked me could only misrepresent my motives and attack my integrity; that they chose to divert attention from the content of my attack by charging me with causing division when I sought a means of partial reconciliation; that they closed their eyes to the reality of the coming agenda by questioning the time-scale I had postulated and ignoring the evidence so clearly before them. The church deserves better than this.

Quite unexpectedly, it became clear that with my sermon I had touched a chord in the hearts of many faithful church people, sick at heart at the direction in which the Church of England has drifted over the past two decades. But we now need greater boldness from those in leadership positions who are sympathetic to a more orthodox faith and practice.

Two months after my sermon, I had dinner with a solid, faithful, evangelical bishop. He told me that apart from the ordination of women (which I anyway set to one side) he agreed with me on every issue I had raised. But had he ever spoken out? I asked. He was thoughtful for a moment. 'No,' he said, 'I haven't. Perhaps I must become more forceful.'

It may be that the more fearful (and who can blame them?) will begin to speak out, and in the process realise that they are not in a beleaguered minority but have the quiet support of the majority of the people – inside and to some extent outside the Church. It will mean that bishops will have to challenge the cosy doctrine of collegiality, by which liberal bishops are allowed to promote their views without check or redress, while the orthodox are persuaded not to break ranks.

Of the clergy, it will – more in some dioceses than others – require courage and boldness to speak out when unorthodoxy is promoted. And those in senior positions must forget the danger it poses to preferment and be ready to support those of us who do choose to brave the heat of the kitchen.

As it happened, I was able to cope without difficulty, but I none the less found it immensely depressing that, in spite of the terrible example of Garry Bennett, I was left almost entirely alone when I faced the big guns of the church's establishment. I was grateful beyond measure to friends and Synod colleagues like Maurice Chandler, Dorothy Chatterley, John Gummer, Jill Dann, Geoffrey Kirk, Peter Geldard and Norah Wilkinson who, without necessarily agreeing with all I had said, gave me their support and assured me of their prayers.

The laity too have a role to play – perhaps the most important of all. The Church of England i a gentlemanly institution, and ladies and gentlemen do not make waves. All too often I am told, 'Of course we don't always like what the vicar says/does/wants. But we don't want to upset him so we go along with it – though most of us don't like it.'

The worm really must begin to turn, not to produce unpleasant confrontation but where possible to ask the clergy to make sure that their people really are with them in what they wish to do. And sometimes, where it is convenient, it may be necessary to find a less uncongenial parish church. Nothing would bring an arrogant priest to his senses more quickly than an appreciable decline in his congregation.

If we, bishops, clergy, lay people, sit back and allow that which we know to be wrong to happen, then we have only ourselves to blame if the Church descends into heresy. But such indolence is an offence against God, for in the end we fight 'not against flesh and blood, but against the principalities and powers of the darkness of this world'.

My life's pilgrimage seems to have given me a small part to play in the present fight for the church's soul. I have never sought it, and would not have desired it. But as I look back over my life, I can see many pointers to the present task. I know that God, who gave me the task when he called me, will furnish me with all I need to fulfil what is required of me.

I have called this book *A Journey to Faith*. It is a journey which has not yet ended and which indeed cannot end in this life, where we see only as through a glass dimly. Our sight of God's glory is obscured by our sins and imperfections as well as by the limitations of our humanity. How indeed could we fully know the One who created the heavens and the earth, from the farthest star to the micro-wonders of matter; who laid the foundation of the earth, determined its measurements, and placed its cornerstone so marvellously that 'the morning stars sang together and all the sons of God shouted for joy' (Job 38: 4–7)?

It has been a happy life, and if I could return to the beginning I would change nothing – not even my many mistakes, for these too have fed my understanding of God's glory. And my sins? Well, there would be sins anyway, and at least I have come to know that God accepts me as I am, warts and all.

And I have much for which to thank God: a delightfully happy marriage, with a kind and generous son and a loyal and loving wife who is also my best friend; a wide circle of folk whose friendship is important and valued and a few special friends who matter even more; and a job which has always given satisfaction and fulfilment as well as a deep contentment.

I know there will be pain in the future. Bobbie and I hope to live long enough to see our grandchildren born and growing, but one of us will die before the other and there will be an emptiness. And since the only certainty for us who have been born is that one day we shall die, friends too will depart beyond death's horizon and we shall be separated for a time – but only for a time, until time is erased by eternity.

There will be pain too in the church I have served for all my adult life. Though we might cry, 'Lord, let this cup pass,' we know it is not our own will but God's which must be fulfilled. The church is the Body of Christ, and although it expresses the joy and certain hope of the resurrection, it is incomplete if it does not also bear a cross.

It is likely – or at any rate a strong possibility – that those, albeit a small minority, of the clergy who in spite of all the pressures to conform remain faithful to Scripture and to the doctrine and practices of the Church of England, will become a church within a church. We shall not leave, for there is nothing in the formularies of Anglicanism that we deny. But we cannot spend all our time and energy in fighting a losing battle against those who seek to undermine faith and Scripture.

I can visualise the day when in retirement I celebrate the Holy Eucharist at my kitchen table because there is simply nowhere else to go. But the prospect for younger orthodox clergy is much grimmer.

Yet my hope is that we shall all stay in the Church of England, whatever the pressures, in spite of the ridicule, and regardless of covert persecution. I could not anyway go elsewhere, for I could not deny what God has done to me and through me in nearly forty years of full-time ministry as a Anglican priest. But *Ecclesia Anglicana* has served this nation for many centuries, and her life is peppered with saints of God who have nurtured the people of England with the truths of holy Scripture and ministered the grace of God to the faithful.

And the faithful remain, decreasing in number perhaps for the moment, yet a remnant from whom will arise a renewed gospel-centred Church of England. The immediate future may be dark, but some time – in ten, twenty, fifty or even a hundred years' time – God will raise up new spiritual leaders who will rediscover truths abandoned, distorted, misused, and ridiculed.

It is our vocation at this dark period in the life of our church to keep the land tilled, quietly preserving the faith, upholding Scripture, teaching the people of God, waiting and praying for the day when under God the darkness of this present world – which seems ready to overcome our church, yet which cannot – is dispelled once again by the overwhelming light of Christ.

In the meantime, God does not call us to be successful, for that is never the Christian's vocation. Rather we are to be faithful – nothing more, nothing less – however dark the way, however painful, however impossible the future may appear.

There is a darkness for our church to face, and I believe God called me into the service of his church those many years ago because he knew my journey to faith would end in that darkness. I do not write that in despair or despondency, for I know that God's truth must prevail, and that others, clergy and laity alike, are there fighting the same battle against the powers and principalities of the darkness of this world.

> For if I say, Péradventure the darkness shall cover me: then shall my night be turned to day.
> Yea, the darkness is no darkness with thee, but the night is as clear as the day: the darkness and light to thee are both alike.
> For my reins are thine: thou hast covered me in my mother's womb.
> I will give thanks unto thee, for I am fearfully and wonderfully made: marvellous are thy works, and that my soul knoweth right well. (Psalm 139: 10–13, BCP)

Now to him who by the power at work within us is able to do far more abundantly than all that we ask or think, to him be glory in the church and in Christ Jesus to all generations, for ever and ever. Amen.

(Ephesians 3.20–21, RSV)

LAUS DEO!

Also published by

TRI∧NGLE

NOT ALWAYS MURDER AT THE VICARAGE
A view of clergy marriage today
by Steve Ann Henshall
Foreword by Eileen Carey

A look at clergy marriage, considering the advantages of
belonging to a vicarage family.

THE GAP
Christians and people who don't go to church
by Jack Burton

Bus driver and Methodist minister Jack Burton describes his
unique vocation ofbridging the gap between two cultures.

FROM NUN TO MUM
An ex-nun adopts twins from South American
by Clare Richards

A personal account of one Christian's journey in faith with a
serious message for the church.

LIVING WITH ANGER
by Myra Chave-Jones

Takes a positive view of anger and how it can be used as an
important part of our lives.

SEVEN FOR A SECRET THAT'S NEVER BEEN TOLD
Healing the wounds of sexual abuse in childhood
by Tracy Hansen

A moving account of a survivor of child sexual abuse
working through the trauma induced by the return of
repressed memories.

PRAYERS FOR PILGRIMS
Compiled by Margaret Pawley
Foreword by David Adam

A unique collection of prayers from different places of pilgrimage in Britain and all over the world, as well as prayers about the Christian life as a pilgrim journey.

SEASONS OF THE SPIRIT
Readings through the Christian year
Selected and edited by George Every, Richard Harries, Kallistos Ware

A rich and varied selection of meditations, poems and prayers from the Anglican, Roman Catholic and Orthodox Christian traditions.

ROUGH WAYS IN PRAYER
How can I pray when I feel spiritually dead?
by Paul Wallis
Foreword by Joyce Huggett

A livey and practical guide for times when personal prayer seems hard.

FROM WHERE I SIT
Living with disability in an able-bodied world
by Alison Davis

A disturbing, personal and often funny account of what it is really like to be disabled.

LIFE LATER ON
Older people and the Church
by Ann Webber

Brings us closer to the experience and insights of older people, describing how they can make up a vital part of most Christian activities.